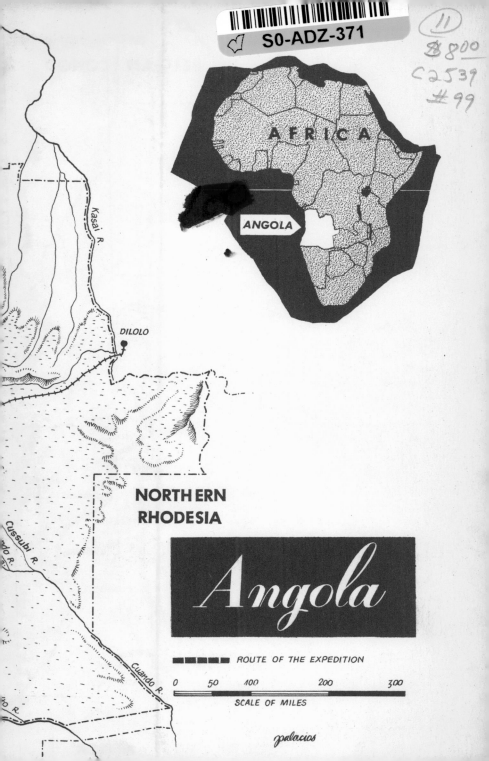

AFRICA

ANGOLA

Kasai R.

DILOLO

Cussubi R.

Cuando R.

NORTHERN
RHODESIA

Angola

■■■■■ ROUTE OF THE EXPEDITION

0   50   100   200   300
SCALE OF MILES

palacios

Doctors, Drums and Dances

DOCTORS, DRUMS and DANCES

by Andreas E. Laszlo, M.D.

HANOVER HOUSE

Garden City, New York, 1955

Library of Congress Catalog Card Number: 55-10511

To Lucille and our children

ACKNOWLEDGMENTS

I want to express here my gratitude to many. Some I purposely leave nameless, yet to them go my thanks in equal amounts. Some, like Brig. Gen. Humberto Delgado, the Military and Air Attaché of the Portuguese Embassy in Washington, D. C., and Dr. Abel Pratas, Chief of Central Commission and Veterinary Service in Luanda, Angola, were vitally instrumental in facilitating my entrance and travelings in Angola. Without their help, I would never have been able to collect material involving intricate and often hidden ceremonies and rites which serve as the major part of my writings here.

Especially Senhores Eduardo Torres and Antonio De Sousa, along with other fine and willing men in Angola, were efficiently plotting my course of wanderings and so directed me to places I would never have found otherwise. For that matter, without them I might very well be stranded and lost somewhere between those rivers, hills, dales and vales.

Then to my good friends in the many missions over there—Dr. Gilchrist, Dr. Tucker, D. Waln, J. Bodaly and Pater Carlos Estermann—I give special thanks. Their sincere hospitality, never-ending care, constant guidance, and the particular help and comradeship of Dr. Gilchrist, joining me on two occasions in the bush, gave me the only chance to see and learn enough to write a considerable part of this book.

Here at home in the States I appreciate the encouragement of my friends, and the diligence of Shirley Sizer, who worked with me for many months on the manuscript. To Doubleday and Company, its staff, and particularly to C. Potter, my editor, goes my sincere gratitude for patience and understanding guidance. And these, indeed, were needed.

Lastly, my heart goes to one who cannot read this book and perhaps will never be aware of its existence—Sunday Joe—the good comrade, and to the other who surely will read it and be very much aware of its existence, I hope—George Wurzburger. Where he left off, Sunday Joe took over!

CONTENTS

9

INTRODUCTION

W HY DOES one go to strange places, wild and lonesome? Why does one expose himself to inconvenience, to being bitten by bugs, to freezing at night, sweating in the daytime, getting hungry when there is only water to drink, thirsty where there is only food to eat, and having thirst and hunger often when neither water nor food can be gotten? I don't know. Some of us are destined to get into trouble like this and still derive pleasure from it.

Horizon chasers. For them it is a challenge to reach for something not within their grasp, and it is more so when their eye cannot see what lies beyond. . . .

Angola is a large, square chunk of country, hemmed in from the north by the Belgian Congo, on the south by South West Africa and Bechuanaland. East of it is Northern Rhodesia and on the west is the South Atlantic Ocean. The Portuguese own it and have managed it ever since one of their intrepid explorers in the fifteenth century discovered it. The theory of assimilation (*assimilado*) between them and the 3½ million natives evidently works well. They have less trouble with them than any nation in any other part of this "dark" continent. There are no more than 70,000 whites in Angola, and in many places the tribes are as remote and little touched by white man's culture and Christianity as anywhere in Africa. Yet the whites prosper fairly well and (more often than not) the blacks are happy and content. Christianity and economic advancement penetrate slowly among them, and consequently they are rarely pulled abruptly from their own environment and left hanging limp in the air, as so often happens in other parts of this vast continent.

For nearly five centuries the Portuguese have been here and have developed a few of the coastal towns into modern and thriving ports, such as Lobito, Luanda, and Mossamedes. They have cultivated the centrally located high plateaus, where, as they proudly state, they can grow sisal, bananas, and coffee, while at the same time a few hundred miles north or south they can cultivate apples, grapes, and blueberries. Cattle can be raised south of the Benguela-Lobito Railway where the deadly tsetse fly is unknown. Diamonds and beeswax are still the principal exports.

Slowly and patiently the missions are teaching the primitive, improving his health and living standard only as he is able to absorb it. Because of this tempo, or perhaps only partly because of it, there is no grumbling and not much friction anywhere. Catholic and Protestant alike, women and men, courageous and stubborn in the belief they preach, bent on a common purpose, first let the native learn how to cultivate the land, how to protect the soil from washing away, let him learn the value of hygiene, medicine, and how to prevent malaria, sleeping sickness, and all the other tropical diseases, teach him to improve infants' and children's chances of survival, and then after give him faith in Christianity.

A strange land about which little is written, but where there is much to see. A land of roaming bands of Bushmen and a place where one can still stumble upon weird ceremonies enacted deep in the bush where the drums are still beating and throbbing, as they did centuries before.

To find reason, cause, and effect in behavior of the primitive, I often found myself presented with his moral, ethical, and cultural problems. Be it sickness, physical or mental aberration, to a physician the fascination of observing and helping is an equal challenge whether it is done amid the conveniences of the modern "gadget age," or under a giant wild fig tree in the bush. There were moments of bewilderment and often no answer could be found, but as an M.D. who is also an agnostic, I had to expect and philosophically accept many puzzling problems.

Most of the persons mentioned here are not fictitious and though at times they are placed in situations not exactly true in reference to their action, deed, or appearance, it is done only to honor them and show the outstanding qualities they possess.

Doctors, Drums and Dances

Chapter I

INTO THE UNKNOWN

T HE BOAT, like a huge, lazy fish, floated gently, anchored close to the north shore on the bronze-hued water of the Congo. Banana Point and Boma—the first sight of African shores—were behind. We passed them in the early morning and kept on fighting the current going toward Matadi. Then we had to stop. Hidden beyond the sharp turn just a few miles away, there she was, like a far cry. The busy port was without enough docking facilities, and we had a four-day wait before she could accommodate us at her quays. On the opposite shore Nóqui, with its few red-tiled government buildings, flashed like a ray of hope through the tropical trees. It made the waiting more tantalizing. Time was precious and by landing at Matadi and entering Angola at Nóqui we hoped to save a week. Little did we know how much more we would lose in the end.

Natives here and there in narrow and dangerously un-balanced dugouts made from tree trunks were fishing close to shore. They handled the throw net well and kept their balance with skill, standing up in those bobbing boats. The current is strong and this mighty Congo is an awful lot of water to fall into, with crocodiles watching every move.

Silently they fished for hours early in the morning and again just before sunset. Then with steady, slow paddling they faded from sight.

The rays of the setting sun reflected on the water and the heat of the ship's steel plates made things hot all around. It was early May, the beginning of the dry season, and the temperature on the open sun deck was in the high nineties. Our truck was brought up on deck from below and we looked it over carefully, checking springs, bolts, and such. In a short time our naked upper bodies, necks and faces, were covered with perspiration.

Finally we arrived at Matadi, and spent two days dispatching letters and telegrams to authorities in Luanda. We needed good will and connections, heading into the unknown.

George Wurzburger from the West Coast, a member of the Adventure Club, had joined me in the States. He is a splendid fellow, a good friend, and reliable comrade who had been in Africa previously, and I couldn't hope for a better man to join me on an expedition. Events proved it, indeed.

Together we started out the next morning at nine o'clock. We had hardly left the town and were still struggling to find the right road leading out from here and toward the Portuguese West African border. The heat was oppressive and I tried to get as much air into the cab as possible. First I let down both windows, then kicked out the ventilator. A sudden cloud of smoke arose. The acrid smell and shower of sparks left no doubt that the truck was on fire. I grabbed the small fire extinguisher attached just behind me on the wall. The darned thing, as most of them do, had a nozzle and a button to push and I never could tell which way that miserable nozzle was directed. I soon found out, however. In great haste I extinguished almost all the sparks of life in my friend, George, practically suffocating him, while the fire fizzled out of its own accord. After both of us recovered sufficiently, George from the fumes of the extinguisher and I from the penitence of my deed and lack of good aim, we started the car again and limped into a garage.

And then the first three hours of this expedition were spent listening to a Belgian speaking French to two Americans speaking no French, trying to explain in deliberate detail what went wrong with the truck. He didn't know what he was talking about and we didn't understand him anyway. Then we had to watch the slow and aimless approach of a native mechanic—our first chance to witness native efficiency—and he never got beyond the approach. At the end of all this it turned out that a wire was cut when the ventilator was pushed to get air into the car and caused a short circuit. Since it could not be fixed, we paid five dollars for nothing more than a lengthy French lesson and away we drove. George's sparkle was missing for a long time.

Nóqui, the entry point into Angola, was only an hour's drive from Matadi, but because of our accident we arrived late in the afternoon. The *administrador* had difficulty in understanding us since he spoke no English and we spoke no Portuguese. The connecting link had to be French. I knew a few sentences such as, "Where is the toilet? Is your father alive? My sister's name is Louise," but strangely that did not seem to be enough. George knew some French too, I found out. He preferred particularly and uttered adroitly again and again with erudite inflection the phrase, "I want potatoes, meat, and coffee." Yet somehow this, too, was not sufficient to expedite our clearance into Angola.

The sun was setting by now, anyway, and our courteous Portuguese friend considered this as a signal to halt his office activities. He suggested we come back the next day. Then he invited us for a cup of coffee. We thanked him for the invitation and George, to carry on a pleasant conversation, repeated the only French sentence he knew. Consequently we got from our host, not only coffee, but potatoes as well.

We returned to Matadi to spend the night.

The following morning we crossed the border again and this time in a few hours, bags, duffles, and all were cleared.

From here on we were entirely on our own, in a strange land and with no knowledge of Portuguese or native tongues. Maps of the country were inaccurate. The best we could find in the States were far from adequate. In his warning the *administrador* at Nóqui explained that, since the rainy season had just ended, practically all bridges were down; but little could one realize how terribly difficult the traveling would be. Bridges really were down, washed away; roadbeds had lost their clay or dust covering, and one found himself constantly driving on boulders and stones. The springs were indeed put to a rugged test. There were neither signs nor indications which way to travel, and if the primitive roads forked, one could never tell which to take. The giant baobab trees, euphorbias, and the lush jungle made the drive scenic, but we saw little game life and few tracks. Large black hornbills the size of turkeys were walking slowly and awkwardly ahead of us in flocks of six to eight. The Portuguese call them *serpentarios,* but erroneously, since they do not actually kill and feed on snakes. The red, bladder-like wattles on their necks showed up grotesquely. It was hard to get near them, so I could neither shoot nor film any. The few primitive villages through which we passed were full of half-dressed, semi-civilized men and women, and bicycles were everywhere. To me nothing looks more slovenly than a native in shirt and shorts, bedecked with all the discarded paraphernalia of civilized life.

This part of Angola is broken up by mountains running roughly north and south parallel with the shore. We arrived at Ambrizete late, in fact very late, having traveled only 150 kilometers on the first day. The small white settlement with its very primitive lodgings gave an initial taste of what to expect. Everything looked desolate, dirty, unkempt, and hopeless. It would have been better to stay in the truck to sleep. We were so saturated with the red-colored dust that it had become a crust over everything. Mosquito nets, sleeping bags, lamps, and food crates all lost their sharp lines, taking on soft and rounded shapes, as though under snow. Trying to find anything in the confusion and disorder of trunks and duffles that had shaken and shifted incessantly loomed like a gigantic task to tackle at that late hour. We decided to look for quarters.

At last in a large, old, medieval-looking building we located a hotel. In the little front room, *bodega,* the owner and his friends were playing cards. Not much attention was given us. The poorly lit, smelly place, the unfriendly reception, and our inability to speak Portuguese did not make matters pleasant. The card-playing ceased and with difficulty it was finally understood that we wanted beds. He led us, with an enormous rusty key in his hand, grunting and talking to himself, toward the back of the building, opened up a creaky, heavy-planked door, and showed us our room, which looked like a sixteenth-century Inquisition cell. The back yard, with high walls and a massive, elaborate entrance, was conveniently shrouded in pitch blackness. So was the room after he left us there. No light, no candle, creaking beds, straw for mattress, and a dirty washstand with one of those tremendous porcelain pitchers resembling a prehistoric bird. And under the bed the proverbial "pot." Lots of foresight and little comfort!

Next morning the *bodega* looked more cheerful and well lighted by sun, but it was equally smelly. At a little table coffee was put in front of us—not too palatable. The bread rolls, hard and generous in size, were good. One could not get butter, but there was olive oil and the eternal sardines. There was sugar on the table, crude and unrefined. I tried to order eggs and attempted to draw a picture, whereupon they brought us two more bread rolls. I gave up and asked for tea.

The going from here was just plain nightmarish. Driving in first and second gear most of the time certainly consumed gasoline. Our mileage estimate was ruined and even the most conservative figures for a day of driving exceeded best efforts. To reach Ambriz with no knowledge of Portuguese, no boy, poor maps, delaying detours, and no signs saying where to go, loomed for the immediate future as a formidable undertaking! And then on top of it, right here and only a few days on African soil, one of those vicious mamba snakes crosses in front of us and I run over him with the truck. That does it—so here again I will have my troubles with snakes! I am afraid of them all and get goose-pimples just talking about them. It makes no difference whether they are garden snakes or diamond rattlers. If anything spoils my pleasure on expeditions to Africa, always it is the snakes. And as it happens, I see more and perhaps have more close calls with them than should be my share.

The last time I was in Central East Africa on an expedition collecting game, I ran into and mostly away from six (6) cobras, I had to shoot one (1) mamba, bludgeoned two (2) puff adders, and each time got scared out of my wits. This is a good deal more snakes than I care to meet. Of course I was assured that I would never see any. I always inquired about them. While planning one corresponds with all kinds of local folk, white hunters, planters, traders, and the like. All wrote back that while living over there and tramping through high and lowlands constantly, they seldom came upon poisonous snakes.

So the first night I was here, under a starlit and beautiful African sky, holding a flashlight, and having to walk only a short distance for an urgent call of nature, what did I run into but a cobra! Imagine, just a few feet away, swaying from side to side with its ugly spread hood, looking straight up at you. That was the end of my urgency.

Those slithering serpents—I had to run into them constantly!

When I crossed through Kruger National Park, I met

Colonel Sandenbergh, the chief warden there. At his supper table, surrounded by his charming wife and children, gruesome stories about snakes were told. But the rangers there always carry serum against snakebites and are ready to administer it in any emergency, so I relaxed. The South African Institute for Medical Research in Johannesburg, with the snake venom received from the Snake Institute at Port Elizabeth and from the Snake Park at Durban, makes up supplies for all public and private needs. It comes in 10 cc. glass ampoules, packed in emergency kit with tourniquet and razor blade or knife for cutting down on the fang wound. So I relaxed more.

There are two large groups of poisonous snakes in Africa. The adder family, or vipers, has a hemotoxic venom, a poison of the blood, dissolving the red blood cells, and creating extensive bleeding in the tissues. Human or animal hit by any of these snakes will in a short time have extensive swelling, bleeding in the local tissues, and later generalized bleeding in vital organs. The other group is the cobra family. Its venom is neurotoxic, absorbed quickly by the nervous system, after which a paralysis takes place, and if the victim has the breath center in the brain paralyzed, he usually dies in a few hours.

So there is a polyvalent serum that protects against both types of snakebite and if given in sufficient quantities, will save the victim. Generally, five or six of those 10 cc. ampoules are needed—one or two injected into the area near the bite, and maybe two or three more used in the course of the next day or so. The only trouble with all this is that no one seems to have more than one or two ampoules and even those are apt to be left behind, either at home, in the office drawers, or in compartments of the car.

So, as Sandenbergh was telling me, one day on his tour of inspection in the northern part of the park, he crossed a heavily wooded and tall-grass-grown section. The natives there are cattle breeders and follow their herds, constantly looking for new pastures. While there checking up on the recent killing of a wildebeest one of his native rangers ran to him to tell that a young boy with the cattle had just been hit by a mamba. It is the most dangerous, unpredictable, and aggressive snake of the cobra family.

He got some serum out of his car and went back to the scene to inject it into the boy. The father in turn refused to allow any serum to be given to the boy. From a little amulet-like wooden container carried on his neck he took a small amount of whitish powder, spat into the palm of his hand, and made a paste of it. He cut down with a knife into the boy's leg just above the knee where the snake hit him, letting the blood flow freely for a while, tied an old piece of rag as a tourniquet on the leg, and rubbed into the bleeding wound some of his paste. The remnants of it he pushed down into the child's throat, forcing him to swallow it by giving milk to drink.

The Colonel felt that the boy had no chance at all since he was small in stature, light in body weight, and the amount of venom from a snake as deadly as the mamba, in relation to the size of this child, certainly must have been overwhelming. He would die in a few hours. Sure enough, matters soon looked bad. He was obviously very ill and became unconscious. So Sandenbergh put him in his car and drove with the father to their hut. The boy had several convulsions en route, vomited, and fell into a deep coma. But to his greatest surprise when he returned in a few days, the boy was still alive. Though very ill and though for weeks only slowly improved, the boy nevertheless recovered.

I wondered just what could have saved that boy and what had happened. The Colonel seemed to think that natives have some efficient concoction or mixture against snakebites. They collect the liver and innards of all kinds of poisonous snakes and lizards. They grind these up, maybe with the snake's head containing the poison sacks, mixing it up with dried leaves and the powdered bark of some particular trees. This they boil and boil for many hours, then let it dry in the sun until a thick mass forms. Then they grind it into a powder that they carry with them always. This must act as an antidote. It certainly proved to be one. The story spoiled my supper and I lost a great deal of enthusiasm for going any farther in Africa. I began to wish that in addition to the serums I carried with me, I could also have some of this strange concoction!

After all, how can one tell?

We had in the jeep truck and carried all through the length and breadth of Angola eight ampoules of polyvalent serum made in France by the Pasteur Institute.

All this, however, didn't change my feeling and dislike of snakes. Here on the road in front of the truck we stood looking over a slick seven-foot, slender as a carriage whip, deadly, venomous black mamba. To be sure, it was crushed to death, but still it made me shudder.

I poked the mouth open to satisfy my curiosity, wedged

a small stick upward, and opened the jaw. The one-and-a-half-inch, slightly curved, needle-sharp teeth in the upper jaw right under the snout, like two glistening silver-white surgical needles, emerged from their sockets: instruments of swift and sure death. Yes, I disliked snakes and silently wondered what I could expect in the months ahead.

We proceeded.

Later I shot a guinea hen, hoping that we could cook it for supper. We passed through a few villages and night caught up with us. George and I debated all day and finally decided not to repeat our previous night's experience, but to stay in the truck on arriving at Ambriz. We could stay fairly close to the settlement, yet out in the country, and make ourselves comfortable in the jeep. We drove so late and so far, however, that to stop somewhere and clear the devilish dust off everything, to set the mosquito nets, and make beds seemed much too much to cope with, so we kept on driving farther and farther, hoping we would reach Ambriz soon.

The road, or path, whatever one may call it, led straight. A single telegraph wire dropping here and there, strung on trees along our path, was the only guide and assurance that we would get somewhere. The road was visible ahead as far as the beam of lights could penetrate.

I was at the wheel and George dozed at my side when suddenly I saw "things" ahead: a large, reflecting, gray, shining surface with white, flowerlike apparitions floating on it.

Suddenly, dead ahead was a massive, swift-running body of water and no road! I just had enough time to jam on the brakes. There was a steep bank and ahead water, water, and water no more than ten feet away. A nice dive under any condition for one who loves being in strange rivers as late in the day as this. George woke with a start, but took considerable time determining that what he saw was not a dream. Where were we? The maps and compass all through the day assured us that we were going in the right direction, but what was this water ahead? The narrow path, wet and soggy along both edges with swamps surrounding it, could not possibly have branched off and the telegraph wire was still with us. The high reeds and tall elephant grass that acted like a wall gave us no chance to deviate. I asked George to get out and look around.

He said, "Okay, but it seems we have quite a few mosquitoes around here."

"What of it?" said I. "For days we've been taking Atabrine tablets. Now is the time to put faith in them. Come on, you just get out."

Poor George! What one friend will do for another. He got out. We each had a Flit gun by now in hand and sprayed a considerable part of this beautiful African countryside thoroughly. But the mosquitoes here were either trained or equipped to withstand such treatment. In no time the cab was alive with them, my shirt, neck, and wrists were covered with the pests, and the last I saw of my friend, he was doing acrobatics, manipulating Flit gun and mashing them in all directions with his handkerchief. He looked like one of those Balinese gods with many arms attached to one body and using them all. Then he disappeared. I grabbed a flashlight and following the strange sounds he made, found him in mud up to his knees and both hands in slime. We could not help but agree that this was water and we were in it. The lovely white things floating on top of it were exquisite water lilies. The swamps were the kind that crocodiles and hippos like. The mosquitoes biting us were doubtless the malaria-carrying anopheles type. In short, nothing was missing to make this situation memorable.

We climbed out of the mud and into the car, and there we deliberated. This did not look like the Atlantic Ocean, for that does not have lilies floating on it. Besides there was no sign of beach, sand, or tide lines. Our direction was southward and we were supposed to be many kilometers inland. Could this be the bight of the river above Ambriz? If so, where was the bridge—the bridge that was definitely marked on the map? Why this abrupt end to the road? There we sat, close to midnight, considerably wet, hungry, and very perplexed. Nothing else could be done but to go back. To turn around, itself, was difficult, requiring some fancy maneuvering in the quagmire.

When we got to a wider and higher part of this seemingly dead-end lane, we had a war conference. Every time we had passed a native hereabout, he had run like mad as soon as we started to slow down. If we could find one now to give information, he would never stand still long enough for it. Even though we could not understand the native dialect, we had to catch one and get our bearings.

"This is the thing to do, George. We passed a village not far back and if you recall, they were dancing there. Let's go back, driving slowly, and see if I can catch one. George, you take over the wheel now and I'll be the catcher."

So we drove back to the village, cruising along in the inky darkness with window down and my arm hanging out, ready to make a desperate snatch.

"There's one—now go steady. There he is. Can you see that shadow? Yes, he's going in the same direction as we are. Now, George, my boy, steady those nerves, don't weaken, just come a trifle toward my side . . . now, watch . . . one . . . two . . . three. Ah! I've got him!"

There was a bloodcurdling yell. Leaning out, I held on for dear life, clutching with both hands his thin, sweaty neck and arm. But he was ours.

"George, I've got him, I'm holding him!"

The jeep truck was stopped. I smiled; George smiled. I patted the poor frightened chap on his face and arms, reassuring him with my best "bedside manner." George shoved cigarettes under his nose. I was ready to sing a lullaby just to quiet his nerves. He was terrified and expected the worst. We dragged him into the car and drove away. The compact proximity of the two races and different colors in the small cab was overpowering. We needed some air. With both windows lowered and the ventilator open strangely enough not one mosquito flew in now that this rich aroma enveloped all of us.

So we drove on and at a safe distance from the village we tried to converse with him. Suddenly I remembered the guinea hen. To pacify him, I could offer that. Assuming a look of unselfish surrender, I handed him the bird for his next meal—he was visibly in doubt that he would ever have another. More cigarettes were held out and dumped on him. No, that was not working either. I talked to him in rapid suc-

cession in English, Hungarian, German and Kiswahili. The
only answer was a garbled, guttural sentence, repeated over
and over. Then George came to the rescue. While I was
holding the boy, offering successively guinea hen, cigarettes,
and whiskey, my friend, my only friend, started to talk in
French. Perhaps it was the smell of whiskey, or maybe even
George's French, but suddenly, as though through an open
floodgate, there gushed forth from our captive the most flu-
ent and long-lasting French explanation. This we could not
understand either, but by using the simple *oui* and *non* we
finally got some idea that we *were* on the right road to
Ambriz. And from the finger-pointing we learned that we
must go back to the marshes. His French certainly came in
handy for us. No doubt he learned it as a mission boy in the
nearby French Catholic Mission.

We turned around, but I would not let this fellow go until
he had come along and shown us how to fly or swim across
that water. He tried to explain something about it, but our
French was insufficient to understand. He was disappointed
at being restrained longer, but grabbed the guinea hen and
so I considered the bargain was thereby sealed. We drove
back, time and time again repeating the name of Ambriz
and pointing into the darkness, and he time and time again
jabbering about something. It was strange.

Once again we reached the fateful shores of the river.
There we stayed and waited. Every so often he yelled loudly
—it could madden a herd of elephants—across the water and
then listened. After a long, long time, just as we were con-
templating throwing him into the water, along with his
guinea hen, an answer like an echo came across from some-

where. After long intervals and an exchange of signals and excited yells the sounds came closer and closer until out of the murky darkness a rickety ferryboat appeared. Three dugouts tied together with ropes and kept afloat on empty gasoline drums with planks lying loose on top came into the beam of our headlights. It was navigated by half a dozen natives pushing and pulling and tugging with long poles, mostly working against each other. But there it was, our rescue and symbol of safe transportation. After a short, silent prayer and the payment of thirty angolares in advance, leaving our friend behind, we drove the jeep truck very, very slowly into the deep, deep, dark nothing, hoping that the wheels would find a groove in which to rest between those sparse, loose planks. I wondered if any insurance policy could cover all this. I don't mind swimming in river or sea if I know where I am swimming. I don't mind swimming if I am among minnows or sunfish, but I dislike crocodiles in the middle of the night in dark water even with alluring lilies around me. I wouldn't like to see our truck slipping into the water, knowing that it wouldn't float. And I wouldn't like inquisitive hippos poking around this misfit of navigation going mostly sideways and seemingly nowhere.

But, *mirabile dictu,* we reached the other side and learned another lesson: When traveling at the end of the rainy season in Angola one shall expect that bridges *are* washed away and should never come to a river unless it is daylight.

Chapter II

THE CUNHAMAS

T HE BEAUTIES of the countryside amply out-
weighed the torture of the road. It was singularly wild in
appearance with huge blocks of rock in every size and shape,
and hilly ground rolling far into the distance with giant baobabs and creepers all around.

South of Dondo, itself a small settlement, only a dozen
or so Portuguese traders there, the roads were almost
entirely impassable, and from there, after crossing the
Cuanza River, the going for days and days was *muito mau.*
I learned one bit of Portuguese thoroughly: *muito mau.* We
heard this often and everywhere. Natives and white men
alike, pointing ahead with many grimaces, emphatically
repeated the phrase over and over: "*Muito mau.*" The exact
meaning of it: *very bad, terribly bad,* or *hopelessly bad.*
For weeks after leaving Angola I had dreams and in them,
like the rhythmic clicking of a railroad train, I heard *muito
mau, muito mau.*

We were constantly fighting the tsetse flies, dreaded
carriers of African sleeping sickness, which, incidentally, is
not the same as what we call sleeping sickness in this country.
Here we call the various types of encephalitis: "sleeping

sickness." The fatal African disease has stood for the past century as more of a barrier against developing many parts of Africa than all the other obstacles lumped together. These longish-bodied flies, the size of a deer fly, will quickly light on arms, hands, or face and any exposed part of the body. Their bite feels like a hot poker. I smeared my face and hands with "dopes" for bugs and mosquitoes, but the tsetse took it as an invitation! Spraying with Aerosol did not affect them a bit. You just had to swat every one of them. There are about thirty or more species and only four or five carry the infection of sleeping sickness, yet these few are quite sufficient to drive terror into white and black alike. And who knows which one is biting you?

Our personal feud with the tsetse was important to George and me. But just imagine what this fly meant and does mean yet to millions in a large part of Africa.

Of the many species of the tsetse only a few actually carry the spirochaeta-infected blood. The worse culprit, known by its melodious-sounding Latin technical name, *Glossina palpalis*, carrying the trypanosoma, in Uganda alone has killed over 200,000 people between 1898 and 1906. This readily gives an idea of what the problem was and still is.

Two different types of organism produce, however, the same sleeping sickness, the *Trypanosoma gambiense* and the *Trypanosoma rhodesiense*. The *rhodesiense* type perhaps responds more successfully to medical treatment.

The same sickness carried by the tsetse, the *Trypanosoma brucei*, called "Nagana," kills in a devastating manner horses, cows, oxen, and dogs and consequently allows no improvement in the economic status and living standard of the native in any of those infested areas when he so badly needs meat and protein for his diet. To eradicate this fly is a fearful problem in its magnitude and it has challenged the ingenuity of the white man for a century now.

The tsetse is a unique insect, asocial, and the only one known among flies to hatch an egg within the abdomen and to bring forth a living larva. While pregnant she needs blood to feed on, and so she carries the infection from animal to animal and from human to human. Fortunately she is not too fertile and her reproduction rate is extremely slow. She does not produce more than about ten young and needs to be fertilized more than once. Their hold on life is precarious and because of it man has a chance against them.

In this fight several methods have been tried. In the Congo the Belgians built a certain type of trap depending on the fact that the tsetse finds its source of food by sight. Setting up over a thousand such traps, they caught about 2 million flies in one month.

The British demarcate large areas where the infection-carrying tsetse is present and by doing so force them to stay there. This fly cannot stand heat and cannot fly far, needs moisture and the protection of foliage, so the government cuts out swaths a mile wide and burns all vegetation in it, including trees and bushes. In that way the fly is restricted to an area from which she cannot fly out and all natives are evacuated.

In the Rhodesias they experimented by killing thousands, perhaps hundreds of thousands of large and small game, trying to eliminate the source of food—"blood pools"—required by the fly.

In the Union of South Africa large-scale spraying with DDT from airplanes and helicopters has been tried.

So goes the heroic human effort to improve land, health, and living in Africa.

George did not feel well. He picked up some tropical "bug" and it laid him low. I tried everything from dieting to stuffing him with various medications like terramycin, vioform, and, of course, all the bismuths.

The first decision to reach Serpa Pinto and from there go straight south and then due east down to the border to Cuangar had to be changed. We found out that south of Serpa Pinto for hundreds of kilometers sand dunes and strange, hostile land without a place to get fuel or water made the plan impossible. Then, talking it over with the *administrador*, to our dismay we found that going to Mavinga, as a second choice, also had to be abandoned.

So we headed southward to Vila da Ponte and continued from there toward Pereira d'Eça. Each day we set out less and less early and less and less brightly. George lived sometimes for days on nothing but a few oranges or on the juice of a cut-open pineapple, but he survived, and we did get south into the country where the Cunhamas live, a large area singularly well suited for cattle breeding.

The *chefe* was not at his post, so where was he? I was told that he had been away for several days collecting hut, or head, tax.

We started following the indefinite imprints of a small car on the sandy and finely powdered ground. A vast expanse of dry, golden-yellow grass stretched endlessly with clumps of thickly grown thorn shrubs and dotted with baobab and euphorbia trees. There are small lakes here, *lagunas*, many miles apart, to attract elephants, rhinos, and all the game. I drove for hours in and out of quicksand, and then reached a small adobe tucked under the shade of the only tree as far as the eye could see. And there was a large gathering of natives. The *chefe* was with them, a young, pleasant-looking chap. He understood some English. We wanted to stay and film the Cunhamas. He was keen and willing and immediately gave orders to his *sepaios,* native policemen. I looked around and there were fine-looking old men waiting silently in a group and looking us over every bit as critically as we did them. These elders came in as representatives from far places and the majority were chiefs of remote villages. After finding out what we wanted they were willing to see that we succeeded.

A serious conference started with much handshaking, oratory, and attentive listening, to the utter delight of them all. They evidently like palavering and much ado and to express themselves walking proudly up and down in front of the others. Each one was a born actor, raising or lowering voice, gesticulating and mimicking to the utmost. I took my camera and started to film the scene. That, of course, meant further embellishments to their rhetoric and gestures. It looked and sounded as if questions of staggering importance were being decided right then and there. It was soon found out that an old chief of a village close to a river intended to fish with his entire retinue, women, children, and men. That was good! Since there was no specific time set, the *chefe* talked him into doing it next day.

Another unexpected surprise came. A tall, strong-looking

young man in a long army overcoat and with a discarded
English bowler on his head came forward and began an
animated discussion about something. The *chefe* explained
that in his village a wedding was scheduled to take place in
a few days. Since the bride would be the first wife of the
bridegroom, a great celebration was planned, many oxen
would be killed, drinking and dancing would go on for
days. He invited us to come. Luck was evidently with us—
fishing next day and wedding a day or so later.

We started out next morning at dawn, having spent the
night at the *chefe's* home. In June the nights are cool here.
It is winter, after all, and the river is cooler. They do not
fish early and it is midday before the sun begins to warm it
up. Around noon a few women came to the banks, tall,
stately figures, unique in the fluid movement of their slender
bodies. They skillfully balanced heavy loads of large woven
baskets on their heads. They looked like experts at carrying
weights in this manner and moved from the hips, keeping
the upper bodies straight. They stopped like timid animals,
then drank, lapping water from their cupped palms. Next in
line a few kids and goats came to drink, tongues lapping
the muddy water.

I was sitting there getting restless watching this pastoral
scene when silently in single file a band of natives came out of
the bush. The old chief we met the day before led, pushing
aside branches of thornbushes, and, behind him, men, boys,
and women. All wore a red and white vertically striped skirt
reaching just above the knees. The women were painted red
over the shoulders, the upper chest, and often on the face.
Their hair was shaved, and their skull formation remarkably

symmetrical and round, perfect in all dimensions with small ears close to the head and only a few decorations in the ears and around the neck. The reddish paint, either an ocher or the powdered bark of camwood mixed with butter or grease, with the blackish glow of the skin underneath, was strikingly beautiful as the sun hit their bodies. A few had a thin leather band over the forehead. It too was painted a brilliant red and each wore a wide, triple or quadruple leather band about the waist, wrapped down and around the upper thighs to secure the skirt. The belt was painted red or blue.

The women carried conic-shaped fishing baskets made of sticks about four feet long. A few of them sat down on the banks and amid laughter and chattering patched, fixed, and checked each. These were comprised of a double compartment, the upper one close to the pointed end, being a trap in which was provided a small opening on one side just large enough for the hand to pass through.

The fishing began. First the men and boys walked into the river, hesitantly, cautiously, and shivering. The pool's width here was about fifty yards. They slowly pushed forward and threw their long, thin spears directly ahead so that the ends sticking out of the silty, murky surface indicated the depth of the pool, thus protecting themselves from slipping into unexpected deep holes. They were walking a few feet ahead of the women, who with much giggling and laughing had gotten into the water too and formed a solid line from bank to bank. The baskets were pushed down with much splashing, open end first, and soon as a fish got caught, the vibration against the hand on the tip of this structure evidently indicated the catch. As one hand held the basket at its bottom, the other, through the small opening at the side, grabbed a wriggling fish and threw it out onto the the bank. There was laughter as the slippery, moistened, glistening bodies churned the water. Crocodiles, if there were any, did not seem to concern them at all. The native is well aware that they will not attack while the thumping, shouting and noise continue. Incidentally elephants too know the crocodiles' fear of noise. I have often seen a herd coming to a pool to drink and the cows not allowing the young to come close to water's edge. They will splash with their trunks, thump, and screech for a while, and then they go in before the young are permitted to drink.

The fishing was over in a short time. The women had done the work and the men paraded ahead and did little, as always. The catch was divided and they left.

That same night I was on the way to the post. It was dark; I did not know my way, of course, and a *sepaio* was with me. We had been bouncing along when unexpectedly we drove into a clearing and came upon a bunch of very surprised young natives. They seemed to be fighting, fighting seriously about something. Driving closer to them, I saw that it was a group of girls, shrieking and shouting excitedly as they beat the stuffing out of a man. The tussle went on. He was down on the ground, covering his head with both arms. In the bright headlights of my truck I saw a regular circus. He tried to fight back, but to no avail. Those amazons got the best of him. I jumped out and ran toward them, but before I reached there they dissolved like camphor, leaving him behind, badly beaten, with cuts on his face.

The *sepaio* came up beside me and with a sheepish grin

tried to tell me something, which, of course, I could not understand. I could hardly wait to get back to the post and there I was told by the *chefe* that at a certain time of the year young girls of marriageable age cover their bodies with ash and roam in a group looking for their former lovers. If they find one and can catch him, they beat him up and take away his knobkerrie—with that he loses the symbol of his manhood. There he had stood, that hapless male all by himself, bruised and forlorn.

Don't underestimate the power of a woman, not even in Africa!

"Another peculiar custom in their love life is the 'bundling,' " the *chefe* continued. "Chipesi, the young Cunhama who is going to be married tomorrow, no doubt had his romantic aspirations and selected his girl, Lufe. She, too, showed willingness for the trial marriage, *tumisa*, and so it was arranged. Lufe went to stay in the hut of one of her girl friends and Chipesi for several weeks visited her there each night."

What went on, what was permitted, how much lure and enticement the *chefe* did not know. But one thing is sure: Lufe saw to it, and likely her girl friend as well, that everything was tried, but nothing succeeded. So early every morning before dawn Lufe returned to her parents' hut and Chipesi, undaunted, tried it every night again and again.

Such will power! Here the end did not justify the means!

But everything went well and after Chipesi collected several goats, one pig, some calico, tobacco, and a few angolares, he visited his prospective mother-in-law. Litigation started in earnest. The gift offered to Lufe's mother greatly helped and finally everyone came to an agreement. Thereafter began a really serious education for Lufe. Her mother and a few relatives, female, gave her a thorough training in "wifely" behavior. As though she ever needed it!

In the meantime Chipesi was feverishly building his own hut, into which they would move after their marriage. The *chefe* with a wink remarked, however, that since the wedding day was so near Lufe's parents looked in another direction while Chipesi and Lufe tried to find out if their love was true.

Next morning from Cafima we headed toward the place where the wedding was supposed to go on. Close to the village I saw four men haggling over something. The chefe roared, the *sepaios* laughed so hard they could hardly hang onto the fenders they were sitting on. This was the final pay-off. With all kinds of gifts those four were reimbursing the bridegroom because the night before, according to the Cunhamas' customs, Lufe, under much ceremonial duress, had to give the names of all men she had ever slept with. Happy days are here again.

Now *there's* a sound economy for lessening the early difficulties of acquiring household furnishings!

Later I got inside the kraal, stockaded as usual. It was complicated and looked for all the world like a crossword puzzle. I turned to the right, I turned to the left, aimlessly walking in a winding corridor flanked with poles on both sides. I circled around granary huts and through a labyrinth of many individual huts of wives. Each had a separate entrance, but all faced toward the chief's personal hut and palaver house. He had seven wives in seven huts. It probably would be easy to steal one of them, but how could one ever find his way out of there? All day I kept getting lost. Whenever I tried to find an exit, I invariably got into a bevy of wives and children. This, at least, was better than being stranded with the livestock, popping up here and there too.

Then several oxen were killed. The old natives did a good job. With light spears, razor-sharp and buttered, they slaughtered twelve of them. Not much time was lost in cutting the meat and apportioned it as gifts to everyone, men and women alike, either residing here or coming from other villages. An ox here is worth 500 angolares, that is about sixteen dollars, so this celebration was a costly and staggering show. The *matabis*—present—was truly overwhelming and Chipesi's father outdid himself.

Not everyone was ready yet. Here and there women stood putting one foot and then the other into a halved gourd, just large enough to hold one foot at a time, and balancing carefully in order not to spill the little water it contained. It showed the importance of the coming affair. After all, in the dry season when rain never falls and there is no river or lake within walking distance, such lavish use of this precious liquid must be for a memorable event. With their finger tips children were painting their own bodies and leather belts in bright reds and blues.

The wedding began by having Lufe, daubed with red on her wide bridal belt, give fire to five old fellows bent with age, holding their pipes in shaking hands. The drummers lined up and two young warriors jumped out, faced each other, slowly circled around, trying to catch one another by the hands. The swaying motion of bodies followed the rhythm of the drums. One pulled the other unexpectedly close and lifted him up in the air, then tried to throw him. It did not work. Ga-ga-eyed children and amused women cheered impartially, screeching and approving regardless of who was up or down.

In one group three of them, like the three Musketeers, were drumming, almost hypnotized. One was especially fascinating. He had a discarded Aussie hat and decorated it with a long, gaudy feather curving like a tail and floating freely in the air, and with it he could well have led a crusade against the infidels. Now and then he would turn suddenly, first to the one on his left and again to the other on his right with palm upturned, outstretched, feinting a thrusting pose and half hiding a grimacing face. In the midst of this acting the two others were so deeply intent beating the staccato that one lost his drum, which rolled away from between his legs, to everybody's delight.

Many dry throats needed lubrication and enormous gourds containing beer and palm wine were everywhere.

Gongoyavo was the medicine man, the master of cere-monies. He had safety pins in each ear lobe; his face was as wrinkled as crepe paper; and he performed a perfect jig dance. Everything in his body trembled with enjoyment, including the safety pins. He hopped up and down, kicking up the white ash with emaciated, bony, chocolate-brown feet. With a stick in each hand he came closer to the group of bridesmaids. Lufe made a good selection—they were all young and plump and very dusky. Every girl held a green-leafed branch as a symbol of fertility in each of her hands. They kept their arms raised above their heads as they danced, slowly, rhythmically shuffling back and forth, but hardly moving their bodies while they jerked their heads up and down. The entire line moved like marionettes controlled by the master of ceremonies, and he, like a giant black spider, leaped up and down and spread his spindly legs in all directions. Certainly no ballet could boast of a better master.

Lufe's bridesmaids were all naked above the waist and wore red skirts close to the body, each held by a wide leather strip daubed with brilliant red paint. But Lufe was dressed in a dark skin skirt and carried a wildebeest's tail like a fly-swatter. She danced for only a short while with her bridesmaids, and then she did the teasing act. She whirled around, disappeared, came back, and moved forward, eyes rolling upward, in every motion of her hips and upper body a suggestion hardly misunderstood, at least hardly so by Chipesi. So he more than willingly came forward, and then only the two danced. Everyone drew back slowly, even the sorcerer.

As the day went by, more and more of them got drunk, but the dancing kept on all through the night. I got dizzy and left.

This Cunhama tribe is certainly interesting—amazing rules and strange customs! For instance, this elaborate wedding ceremony is enacted only with the first wife. A marriage of this kind will always take place about twelve days after the bride menstruates. Usually that is when she ovulates, which is the likely time for conception. A child in marriage as early as possible is much desired. The more children, the more wealth. So Chipesi, whatever he paid for Lufe, borrowed it from brothers, fathers, and his mother's relatives. And now from this initial investment he will strive hard to pay back his debts and mushroom his possessions and wealth by begetting child after child. His daughters will bring him back livestock when he sells them and his sons will help to safeguard and increase it when they watch over it. As he becomes established, his dividends accrue. The wealthy Cunhama is still able to allow himself more than one wife, and the headaches with them.

The current price of a bride in this vicinity was two blankets, eight yards of cloth, one belt, a headcloth, a large or small hog, and six chickens—a sizeable swag—all this returnable if she proved to be sterile. Or maybe a younger sister would be acceptable in exchange. So Lufe had to prove her worth.

At present their changing economic environment inevitably makes them lean toward monogamy. Missionary teachings, Christian concepts of family units, partly are the cause, but not to the extent that one likes to believe. The native might accept the monogamous state at first without any conviction, since it can be an advantage to his economy, but not because it improves his morals. Besides that it does not solve the problem of the preponderance of females in the tribe. There is an ever-present surplus of them and, according to their moral code, the free-floating woman simply selects a man by going to his hut of her own volition and stays with him there. He builds her a hut later and thus she is accepted, joins the unit as another wife, starts to work for him and bring forth children. Prostitution and promiscuity are little known.

In a community such as this where the rules were, or are, based on needs of its members, everything will run pretty smoothly until foreign ideas and strange laws upset this equilibrium. Apparently their conduct is not haphazard. On the contrary, it is well calculated and the result of reason and purpose. Polygamy is not an immoral act, but an economic necessity. In the faraway bush country where there is hardly any contact with the white it will change only as the emancipation of the primitive woman takes place. She is the "beast of burden" and her lot is hard and her endurance taxed to the utmost. She is the one who tills the ground and toils on it from morning to night. The miserable return of a small mound of beans, manioc, maize, and sweet potatoes grown in poor soil must feed her, the children, and her husband from one season to the next. The man does not work, seldom hunts, and certainly does not put himself out to assure food for his wife and children. It is the woman's chore and her responsibility. Therefore, more wives mean more hands to work and polygamy provides an answer. The more contact a tribe has with the white, the more likely that they will absorb, imitate, and desire to possess some of the comforts resulting from his civilization. With that comes better methods of soil cultivation and more agricultural products. It gives the primitive a better chance to possess a plow instead of a hoe, a pair of oxen instead of three extra wives. The tribes deep in the bush will learn this later. The wild and shy ones, influenced more by the medicine man than by the missionary, will come to this slower. Therefore, it is slowest with the Bushmen and the Cheokwees, and less so with the Cunhamas and Huilas. Polygamy is almost completely dropped among the Ovimbundu.

And so changes will take place and Christian principles will be wholeheartedly adopted, according to geographical location and proximity to the white.

Chapter III

DISCOVERY IN THE DESERT

T HERE IS no limit to what a Portuguese will do for you. In Luanda, Dr. A. Pratas, head of the Veterinary and Game Department of Angola, a gentleman and an outstanding sportsman, gave me every courtesy and assistance, and far in advance made arrangements for the co-operation of governors, *administradores*, et cetera. Senhor Eduardo Torres was alerted to pending plans and advised to join us in the expedition to the southwestern part of the great Angolan desert bordering on South West Africa.

From Sá da Bandeira to Mossamedes there is a gradual decline from an approximate elevation of six thousand feet to sea level and the road winds around on the hairpin turns of the mesas and escarpments. We got to Mossamedes, we found Torres, and matters progressed smoothly from there on.

After a few days of preparation we started out. The jeep truck, with canvas canopy, heavily reinforced in the rear and underneath, carried foam-rubber mattress, guns, films, cameras, and a certain amount of food. Mosquito nets were tied on the supporting bars. The truck held thirty gallons in its tank, but the quality of the gasoline was poor. The extra twenty gallons of gasoline we carried in cans often turned out to be much less than we needed on this roadless, sandy, and rocky terrain. The large amount of sugar produced in Angola is fermented into alcohol and it is more profitable for the government to mix it with the gasoline than to export it. This mixture gave us plenty of trouble. It didn't have much power, was consumed fast, and chewed through the fuel-pump gasket, leaked, and the gasket had to be replaced every five thousand kilometers. Senhor Torres had an open-type army jeep and carried an extra barrel containing sixty gallons besides his jerry tanks. So with the two trucks, at least a certain amount of mobility was assured.

The traveling was fair on the hard-packed, sandy surface for the jeep and jeep truck, packed to the gunwhales and our boys hanging onto ropes for dear life. Torres looked like a determined matador attacking the empty space ahead. There were no roads and no markers; the high tableland stretched endless and barren, sparsely dotted with low shrubs and thornbushes. Occasionally we changed cars and as I was driving the open jeep, I saw a lesser bustard take flight, flushed by the approach of this caravan. I was having enough trouble trying to maneuver the truck among anthills, wart-hog holes, and stumps. At times I went to the right and then to the left, easing the jeep into holes with one wheel, and with others up in the air. I found myself going in neat circles just to avoid some obstacle and totally sepa-rated far away from the other car. I decided to look for an antelope. I had to shoot something anyway since we had no meat.

My gunbearer boy sat at my side with the double-barreled .470 between his knees for emergency. A shotgun was danc-

ing up and down between us, and though it was tied in a
sling, with that "up and down" nothing stayed put. One
must always have ready a heavy rifle and a shotgun, the
latter for birds and snakes.

I saw something moving ahead in the bush. I could not
be sure whether it was an animal or my vision was playing
fantasies with me. Mirage was constantly ahead and beyond.
The small growth of African scrub oak and the thick, low
thorn trees closed here and there around us like a well. I
kept on driving, holding onto the wheel with both hands and
scanning the ground. Again a few hundred feet ahead something black seemed to move. What was it? My boy, too,
watched it, alert, body stiffened like an animal with wide
nostrils in that flattened black nose, eyes glued. At first I
thought it was a wildebeest or maybe a springbok. A keen-
eyed native boy, a hunter by instinct, sees much that lies
ahead and would know better what to look for.

I stopped the jeep, picked up the glasses hanging from
my neck, and carefully surveyed each group of trees, leaving
not one unobserved, and watched for motion. I spotted a
grayish black mass melting so well into the shade of scrub
trees that I could not tell what it was, waited with glasses
fixed, but no motion, no action took place. I dropped the
glasses and was just trying to decide whether to drive on
or wait when the boy touched me lightly and gripped the
rifle, pushing it slowly toward my side. He saw something
with the naked eye that I could not see well with glasses in
that haziness. I looked again and this time saw what I thought
was a horn on the gray, shapeless form. It looked like one of
the horns of a rhino. In what relation this was to his head, if

it was the front or the second, rear horn, I could not discern. By now I was reasonably sure that it was a rhino, but I could not tell in which direction he faced. Was he feeding or watching, was he lying down or standing ready to give us trouble? It is strange that unless a game moves a part of its body, often in spite of close range and powerful glasses, one cannot tell what one actually sees.

That stupid rhino! They all are stupid, anyway, and just how unpredictable and cussed this one was there was no way of knowing. His eyesight is poor, so he sees little or nothing. Besides that, those horns sitting on his nose probably make him cross-eyed. His ears are small and stuck on his head in the wrong place, so he hears little and what he hears is evidently beyond his comprehension. But his nose is big and he surely can smell with that. If it were not for the tick-birds, his best friends, giving him warning of any danger or approach, he perhaps would wander about and fall into some big hole and snort, snort, snort again. That he does damned well.

At any rate there he was, thinking it over only 200 feet ahead. Or it may be that he cannot think. Perhaps he did not even know we were there. I had no intention of hunting rhino. I decided it would be best to ignore him and go downwind and not molest this "baby." So I slowly put the jeep in gear and attempted to get out of the hole into which the front wheels had settled. I am sure that the noise of the engine, the creaking axle, and groaning body would have awakened the dead. I was still partly in the hole when his tickbirds flew up and fluttered, their shrill cries giving him a definite sign that something was close and coming.

Those birds! They live on his ticks and remain on him while he supplies the food for them. They, in turn, make sure that nothing happens to him—an equitable arrangement. Each of them must have a number of those special friends, special tickbirds, and so, if he runs short of ticks to supply them, I imagine he would go into the bush just to get more on his hide. Thus everyone is satisfied: the tick gets his blood, the bird gets his ticks, and he gets rid of them, feels better for it, and at the same time has his personal alarm system.

So those birds had done it. The warning was sounded and trouble was bound to start. I had little time to think, for he came like an avalanche, breaking bush and trees, and took the shortest and straightest line for the jeep. Those funny little ragged and ripped ears with the small hair tufts were stretched forward and his little tail was up and rigid. This two tons of cussedness, this stupid, snorting fool, may have thought that my jeep was another of his own kind with whom he wanted to settle something. I knew that charging idiot, if he kept on, would hit the jeep head-on and overturn it.

The motor stalled; we were still in the hole. I grabbed the gun. I *had* to turn him. Aiming at the base of his horn, I hit the mark, hoping that I gave him an awful headache. He stopped as if hit by a bulldozer, and then turned. The shock of the bullet hitting with 3000 foot pounds of energy was enough to change his direction. "He's going to fall," I thought to myself as he wobbled and acted dizzy. But no; with much grunting and snorting slowly he turned and trotted away, disappearing in the bush to the left of the jeep.

I breathed deeply and, relieved, grinned toward the boy.

He took the rifle and reloaded it immediately, still very alert, not smiling at all, just looking ahead and watching. He did not trust the situation and knew better the unpredictable, stubborn idiocy of our horned friend. I turned the glasses toward the bush where he had gone and saw him there sulking all by himself.

I started the engine again.

Gradually we pulled out of the hole and had just picked up speed when that blooming fool decided to start the show again. He could not get our scent, though this time we were upwind from him. The jeep, with oil, gasoline, and rubber mixed with the human scent, I am sure was too much for him. He thumped the dusty ground and snorted.

Head down a bit, with those little bloodshot eyes, and puffing like a freight train, he came at us, attacking this time from the side. I really did not want to kill him—I would have to try to turn him once more. The problem was where to aim and shoot so as not to wound him too severely. He gave me no chance to ponder. Closer and closer he came, larger and larger he loomed.

I seized the rifle and aimed at the base of his horn again. He ran sideways with those short, funny, bucking jumps as I shot and missed clearly. Turning my body hastily from the wheel and shooting quickly, I must have shot high.

Before I knew it, he was right close, awfully close, just a few feet away from the jeep. Now he really meant business.

I shot again, to kill, got him just behind the right front leg and high in the shoulder. On he came still, staggering and weaving, and with a last effort rammed his front horn straight into the fender, turning the car over and sending my boy and me flying.

There he was, dead rhino, spiked into the front fender with horn locked, and stretched out in eternity. The engine was still running.

Stupid rhino!

The sound of the shots helped Torres to find us and soon brought him to the scene. With the assistance of the native crew we got the jeep back on its four "feet" again. No one was interested in rhino meat, so we went on.

We traveled several hours without interruption, averaging thirty to forty kilometers per hour. I noticed here and there a peculiar-looking plant. The giant double leaves, facing each other but curled up, were parched, yellowish, and wilted. To me they resembled so many dried-out, sickly cacti. The thick, woody center part was loosened from its root and looked truly pathetic. We had entered the area of the *Welwitschia mirabilis,* reputed to live for a century. There were hundreds and hundreds of them extending to the very horizon like so many huge spiders lying flat and close to the ground. It is the only place in the world they exist.

We went on. More dust was churned up and swallowed. Torres's jeep, like a grasshopper, jumped up and down in front of us and by now our boys, sitting on the luggage-filled rear platform, looked as though they had turned into a couple of anemic apparitions of a dusky tribe. The silvery, chalky, fine volcanic dust, mixed with the sharp, small, gritty sand in the air, covered them from head to foot. How they could ever breathe in those dust clouds was a wonder. In the distance large granite boulders loomed up. They were thrown over each other like so many smooth-surfaced round balls or giant squares. Each group was sharply silhouetted, and as we passed them close by I noticed some sparse grass and bush vegetation growing in the vicinity. There must have been moisture around to account for this vegetation. I stopped, picked up my shotgun, got out of the jeep, and went closer. Climbing onto a group of boulders, I found a small tanklike area in the rock, covered and protected by overlapping giant rocks, with some brackish water in it.

Heading back, I spotted a flock of guinea hens and walked toward them. A guinea is larger than our ordinary hen, easy to cook, and is very tasty, so I never miss an opportunity to hunt them. But they have the annoying habit of running, running, running, and seldom take to wing unless rushed, so I had to keep running, running, running after them. It is unsportsmanlike, but if you need them for the pot, it is much to the point and effective to shoot them on the ground. Just blast into them with both barrels, hoping to hit as many as possible.

And I was right on the verge of doing this when I heard a hissing noise and instinctively stopped. I froze and felt every drop of blood in me chill. Practically under my feet in the not too high and dry grass I saw a slightly coiled-up, five-foot long, beautifully colored, ugly death staring into my eyes. I was so surprised and scared at the same moment that with the gun in hand I stood transfixed and just did nothing. Before I could realize it, he hit and though I was more than five or six feet away I felt I was reached somewhere on my right foot above the ankle. I shot and shot again, never aiming, never knowing. How I hit him, how I killed him, I don't know, but it was more than I bargained for.

I was certain I had been bitten, yet totally unable to sense or remember if I felt pain or sting. With the snake shot literally to pieces in front of me I bent over and frantically searched on my foot and leg for fang signs. There were none. As I checked on my twelve-inch-high shoepack, just an inch or so below the top, right over the heavy brass hook and where my Bean shoelace was in a double knot, I found the deep cut and fang mark completely penetrated through the elk-leather top, but slid down during its stroke because of the brass and thickly bunched leather. It was not my moment to die.

It was a Gaboon viper, a lethal and much-dreaded snake, rather sluggish, but beautifully marked with brilliant red and blue spots, a member of the adder family. All my serums would have been of little use if I had been hit by him. He is the rare snake with the combination of venoms that kills by paralyzing the nerve system as well as destroying the red cells.

Then and there I gave up my guinea-hen hunt.

When I got back to the jeep I mentioned nothing. Torres asked what I had shot at.

"Was it a rhino?"

"No."

"Was it a springbok?"

"No, it wasn't."

"Were they guinea hens perhaps?"

"No, they weren't guinea hens."

"Then what in hell did you shoot at?"

"Oh, it was only a Gaboon viper. Let's get out of here."

That night we camped close to a spring and could conserve our precious water supplies. The cooking was simple. We opened cans and over a fire we boiled our coffee. We bedded down while hyenas and lions serenaded through the night, I in a sleeping bag and Torres on his straw-filled mattress.

Early in the morning we made breakfast and Torres remarked that three years before, while hunting here for elephants, a Herero tribesman guiding him spoke about some strange rock carvings. It was Torres's conjecture that some fetish or superstition was connected with it, since the nomadic natives kept away from that large granite hill. He had been led there and found some inexplicable hieroglyphics. We decided to head for the hills and search for the carvings.

Granite hills of different heights, basalt-like formations, and occasionally some rotted mica mountains loomed up toward the south. By now we were ranging closer to the main massives of the Serra da Chela. The elevation here was about 1500 feet and the peaks of those desolate and craggy ridges were between 5000 and 6000 feet. Traveling became extremely difficult. Something was wrong with the right-front-wheel drive and its packing. There was a knock in it when turning, although at Sá da Bandeira before starting to Mossamedes the jeep was carefully checked. Portuguese mechanics are inclined to be lackadaisical, and though they had removed the wheel and repacked it, the knock had returned. We had to use the front-wheel drive in this territory anyway. Often in sand up to the hub and repeatedly in narrow, dry river beds strewn with rocks and boulders, we were obliged to drive in low gear. The sand all but stops you. You slowly drive into the donga, losing momentum until you are nearly at a standstill as you start to climb the other side. It is a slow pull. The jeep is groaning and grinding underneath and you are groaning, cussing, and praying, wondering why in God's name you ever started and what made you choose this place anyway.

Torres, with the uncanny ability of a terrier, after circling and backtracking finally located the hill.

We stopped under the shade of a large acacia before we started to climb the hill. The east side of it was smooth. An approach on its western face was practically impossible. The hill was approximately 900 feet high and after climbing halfway we came upon the carvings, on the eastern side. There were various figures, some like a sun with rays, others like a centipede, and generally similar to Egyptian hieroglyphics. I counted over fifty of them in a square some 200 yards wide. Over the centuries erosion, wind, rain, and changing temperature have scarcely lessened the depth of the grooves. How old are they? How were they made? By what people, wandering or permanent inhabitants of this spot hundreds or thousands of years ago? We had no answer.

Later we ran into a group of American and Canadian geologists out in nowhere. They had a base camp close to the border where South West Africa and Angola meet, and they were in the midst of several months' study of the local mineralogical conditions. When far in the distance we sighted red and yellow trucks neatly lined up beneath a few giant trees nesting against a mountain slope, my heart sang. There I was able to wash, see water and drink it with confidence, to eat, and then listen to a short-wave radio, which made things rather tolerable, scorpions, snakes, and sand flies notwithstanding.

Next morning we headed straight south to locate Iona, the only port in this sea of sand. It is a small, whitewashed structure with a stone veranda looking toward the steep and tremendous mountain slopes. There is a garage affair built by the Americans to service their own equipment, jeeps and what not. This little spot of civilization under the relentless sun is hewn out of stones with a few miserable planks put together to serve as a garage, which was nothing more than a crude, airy, square hut without side walls, but with a roof made from freshly cut branches of trees, leaves left on them to act as insulation from the heat. Fuel and oil were available and because of the kind assistance of Dr. Robertson, the chief geologist, an American mechanic was available. This young mechanic, looking over the jeep with his .45 Colt hanging at his waist and a monkey wrench in his hand, diagnosed the trouble. His assistant, a Portuguese mechanic, didn't do much assisting. He spent all his time keeping his pet monkey away from the monkey wrenches. At any rate the trouble was found and it turned out that, instead of putting a heavy packing grease in the front-wheel bearing, in Sá da Bandeira they used Valvoline motor oil. *Voilà!* Have a good time in southern Angola!

Chapter IV

SUNDAY JOE

AT SÁ DA BANDEIRA we arrived completely played out after hard days of traveling north. Circumstances forced us to stay. The jeep truck again needed servicing and rechecking; the front wheel had to be taken off. We both were in need of more than one hot bath to scrub off all the dust. It is amazing how much dirt one collects in Africa.

A good deal of deliberation and planning went on again. George's indisposition persisted. The question was whether to go back south and explore roughly the desolate area between Chibemba and Mossamedes, or to go more northerly and to Nova Lisboa, from there take a train, putting the jeep on it, and head eastward. My only concern was to see as much as possible of this unspoiled virgin land and its never-written-of, little-known primitive tribes. It was finally decided to take the northern route.

At Nova Lisboa serious trouble arose. George became really ill and, distressing as it was to us both, it was necessary to make a final decision. I fully realized that unless I assured him that I could go on alone, he would stubbornly stick to our original plan. Convinced at last that he should give up, with heavy heart he boarded a plane and flew back to the States. His condition was never fully diagnosed, but I think he had amoebic dysentery.

So, left alone, I realized that, besides the usual retinue of hired natives, porters, and the like, I must have a *personal* boy. Little did I know about the mechanical problems of the jeep truck and if a tire had to be changed, or a spring broke, or if I got stuck on those difficult roads and tried to pull myself out, I certainly would need assistance. This careless and seemingly haphazard way of going into the African bush was, and still is, a characteristic trait of mine. Maybe I am stupid, or perhaps a fatalist, possibly both. But since I have no time to study mechanics, nor the inclination for it, I skip such trifles, embark on a blissful adventure, and let the devil take the hindmost. I did not speak the native language. Umbundu is entirely different from Kis-wahili, some of the latter of which I had learned in my previous wanderings over Central East Africa. This area was entirely new to me and the best I could do was use sign language, but two hands and two feet were not enough to convey all I wanted to say. I had to get a boy.

The prime requisite was, of course, to speak at least enough Portuguese and English between us so that we could understand each other. As it turned out, selecting a boy was more difficult than I anticipated. Any number of boys are available, but most of them useless. It is entirely a matter of luck whether or not one gets a boy who is both serviceable and faithful.

One clear, bright morning I drove the truck to the office of the Companhia Mineira de Lobito, which is a joint venture involving some very influential Portuguese and an American mining corporation. Several American and Canadian geologists, very pleasant fellows indeed, were in the midst of organizing the whole enterprise, and hiring and firing many of the Portuguese and natives as well. There I found a large assortment of natives who gathered every morning to wait for odd jobs. Quickly glancing over the group, and guided by fate alone, I selected one brightly smiling, fairly well-built and clean-looking boy. I stalked boldly toward him, grabbed him by the shoulder, shook him hard, and as he still kept on smiling, I considered he had a sense of humor and a degree of courage and physical stamina, too. I began explaining in lengthy English how much I needed him and how important a person he would be on my safari. He was an exceptionally bright chap and seemed to understand me fully by assuring me with a Portuguese *"Sim, senhor"* that everything would be all right. I knew the exact meaning of *"Sim, senhor"* since it was the bulk of my Portuguese vocabulary. The only indications of his comprehension of what I was trying to tell him were his bright eyes, his willingness, and his short reply of *"Sim, senhor."* From here on I knew we were going to get along famously. We exchanged only a few words in the weeks ahead and even those were not understood by each other. It was a question of operating together by sheer intuition and a joint willingness to place our lives in the hands of fate as we headed into the unknown.

So I pushed and pummeled him into the cab of the truck while reassuring him that henceforth he would be well taken care of. I explained that for many weeks he would be accompanying me and that if he had any family, wife or children, or children but no wife, for that matter, he could rest assured that someone would take care of them in his absence; whereupon he said, "*Sim, senhor*." I asked him his particular liking in food and drink. I went into a lengthy monologue on the relative value of Portuguese red wine compared with the white. He responded with a hearty "*Sim, senhor*." Then I went into a store where I bought a water canteen, half a dozen cans of sardines, several bunches of small native bananas, and showed them to him proudly, assuring him that in the future he need not worry about dying of hunger. He answered me again with "*Sim, senhor*," and promptly took out a piece of rag in which was wrapped a small, whitish mash which turned out to be ground-up maize, and offered that to me in turn. That was my cue to answer, but I did not say, "*Sim, senhor*."

Being anxious to start out that very morning, I fueled and checked the truck and set out toward the Dondi Mission with my boy beside me. I decided to visit the mission in Bela Vista in order to meet a well-known Canadian missionary doctor there, visit the Leprosarium, look over the mission's medical work and get some further information and advice for my expedition south. Bela Vista from Nova Lisboa is about eighty-odd kilometers. A fair road minimized the risk and made this seem the perfect opportunity to try out my new boy, to find out if the truck was in good shape, and to get generally organized for the much tougher and much longer trials ahead.

After a couple hours of bouncing up and down and going in all directions but the right one I discovered that my boy was more valuable than I had realized. He knew the road to the mission. Had I been alone where no directional signs are posted, without a doubt I would have landed in some spot far from my intended destination. However, fate was good to me and around noon we arrived at the mission. After I found Dr. Gilchrist and introduced myself to him, I asked if he could communicate with my boy, explained to the doctor that I had a newly acquired boy whom I was taking on a several months' safari, and added that I knew absolutely nothing of him or his tribal affiliation, but only that he had bright eyes, a pair of questionably clean white trousers, an old discarded U. S. Army jacket, and a willing heart. When I announced that I did not even know the boy's name, the good doctor looked a little surprised, but, being Anglo-Saxon, always kept his emotions under control and with a great dignity turned to the boy and asked for his name. Thus I learned my boy's name is José Domingo (Sunday Joe). Well, that suited me and certainly suited him.

In the course of subsequent conversation I also found out from the doctor that my boy had been in the Portuguese Colonial Army. That must be why he always stood at attention and for some devilish, unknown reason was continually polishing everything he could put his hands on. He polished my truck outside, he polished it inside. He polished my shoes, sometimes even my toothbrush. He polished my eating utensils, and he polished off a large jug of my Portuguese red wine. That immediately made him so happy that he drained the oil from the crankcase and put so much water into the radiator that it promptly boiled over. He was a delightful chap and those were only the early trials and tribulations of our lasting friendship. We grew

closer to each other with more and more understanding,
which was entirely spiritual, without vocal manifestation.

As the weeks passed he definitely adopted me as a decora-
tion in his life and an advantage in his relations with the
other natives wherever we went. I suspect he exhibited me
as his prize possession, his badge of distinction. What he
actually said about me I shall never know, but his delivery
contained an abundance of gesticulation, change of voice,
and intonation. I must admit that most of the time his
technique worked sufficiently to enable me to photograph
and film many scenes among primitives that otherwise might
have been impossible. He learned quickly how to handle and
carry the cameras and, as I have so often noticed with natives
who had no previous training in the use of mechanical
contraptions, he was very deft with his fingers and hands, and
many times recognized by just listening to the sound of the
humming mechanism in the movie camera whether or not
the film was stuck, or slowing down, and then he was right
on hand, ready with an extra magazine.

José possessed a natural artistry and diplomatic talent
for smoothing the ground of approach between the natives
and me whether on the roadside or in the bush or elsewhere.
Many of those natives are extremely shy. Perhaps it results
from an inborn fear, a distrust of the white man; perhaps it is
based on past experience; or it may be simply a tribal taboo,·
but often even slowing down the truck when I came across
natives somewhere in the bush was sufficient to make them
run like so many rabbits and evaporate into thin air. Without being able to explain this situation to José we worked
out quite a smooth and successful *modus operandi,* which

we employed in unison. When unexpectedly we approached
a scene or any group of natives I wanted to study and film,
José knew it merely by watching the gleam in my eyes. Then
when I carefully slowed the truck he grabbed a handful of
cigarettes in one fist and some glass beads in the other and
at the strategic moment leaped out of the moving truck
like an enormous bat. Before the surprised natives even had
a chance to get a good start, he descended upon them, wildly
throwing the cigarettes in every direction and shoving the
multicolored glass beads under the eyes of the fair sex.
What he told them is a mystery to me, but apparently he had
a fine story about me, because when I finally got out of the
truck, usually they all were willing at least to stand their
ground.

So that was Sunday Joe. He took good care of me, indeed.
He didn't polish me outside and inside as he did my truck,
but he watched out for me at night, he set my mosquito nets
over my bedding in the truck where I slept, he built fires
and boiled water for my shaving in the morning, he kept my
maps and notes in a place where I could find them (and much
better than many of my secretaries in the States). Perhaps
at times he overplayed the role of guardian angel, but if so,
he did it from the goodness of his heart.

Chapter V

DONDI MISSION AND THE LEPERS

Tᴴᴱ ɴᴀᴛɪᴠᴇ in Africa has a life expectancy only half the average of the white man's in the United States. Yet he does not drop dead unexpectedly of coronary thrombosis while phoning from his comfortable armchair. Surely he has none of the humdrum activities of our daily living, but on the other hand might have to face a marauding or charging lion and, while doing so, be chewed up. Both that and all else that comes to him in his daily living, as danger or surprise, he can stand. He is stolid, patient, and expects little from life, therefore, still has his humor and ability to laugh, dance, and play the drums. That surely saves his blood vessels, and most likely he will not die of a heart attack. He needs no adjustment of personality, he is not frustrated, and above all, he is not neurotic and insecure as we are in spite of all our possessions and gadgets that make us happy. His diet is deficient and heaven only knows why he has any strength to exist since he takes neither B complex nor wheat germ! The poor guy has no radio to tell him in what constant danger he is by neglecting to take his Carter's Little Liver Pills.

As the frantic search continues for an answer to the much

too early and increasing number of hardened arteries in
heart and brain and kidneys of the white and civilized, a
clue might well be found in the philosophy of the African
native. The solution to this very real and grave problem
of modern medicine—arteriosclerosis—may lie in studying
and applying the correct approach to the basic essence of life,
and not in the counting of fat molecules under the ultra-
high-powered microscope. Less sitting through our days,
weeks, months in comfortable offices with intercommunica-
tion systems at our fingertips, less automobile driving with
power drive, power steering, and built-in automatic devices
for scratching our nose and ears, less "rat-racing" and less
competing against our "brothers" might give us slower and
therefore more normal heart rate, better blood circulation,
and so a likely chance to live longer.

Here in the narrow corridors of this simple and strongly
built hospital at the Dondi Mission I walked toward a small
room. Shafts of light came in through the few windows on
one side. There was the modestly outfitted laboratory
with roughly hewn tables, microscopes, knives and forceps,
chemicals, and stains for tissues. It contained the most
essential but simple paraphernalia of modern medical science.
The two native assistants, trained by the mission's white
doctor in elementary laboratory techniques, were working
here, hardly bothering to look up and notice me. A male
native nurse held a safety-razor blade and with quick, deft
motion removed a small piece of skin from the horribly
mutilated face of an old woman who stood there during this
operation in a stolid and resigned manner. Evidently she
had no sensation of pain. One type of leprosy, this awful

affliction, will make parts of the body, fingers, hands, face, completely numb to pain or touch. The nerve endings are blocked, no impulse of sensation will ever come through— nature's way of anesthetizing.

The small piece of skin, scaly, almost transparent, was then prepared, put on a glass slide, and stained with a specific fluid to find the leper bacillus. A case of leprosy proven again. Under primitive conditions a constant search continues for early or advanced undiagnosed cases in order to separate them from others and thus prevent the spread by contact. The little that is known is used to do the most. Unheralded but utmost, determined, human, heroic effort is going on here all the time.

Leprosy—this strange and old scourge of mankind, the Biblical disease, a never-solved puzzle to medical minds. It is caused by a bacillus, *mycobacterium leprae,* very, very closely related to the bacillus of tuberculosis. Under the microscope and with the method of staining to recognize its shapes and characteristics, it is like a brother to a sister. Yet in its manifestations on the human body it is vastly different from it. It does not affect the lungs. It is a slowly progressing, inevitably advancing infection that, up to now at least, cannot be transmitted to lower animals in laboratories. It enters the human body in an unknown way and it might harbor there for ten to fifteen years before showing its first signs of damage and incurable ravage on men, women, children, and the old alike.

Missionaries, doctors, nurses, and nuns working among those unfortunates might contract it, and again many living among them all their life will escape it. Why? No one seems to know. There are over 4,000,000 of them in the world and more than 40,000 in Angola alone. It is not a disease of the tropics exclusively. Men have it in Norway and in Iceland, as well as in Wisconsin, New York, and again in Africa. In the Middle Ages chains of hospitals were built all over Europe to isolate and confine them. Everyone feared this horrible disease. It was a mess, frightening, with nightmarish consequences. Then within the short span of a century it disappeared from there almost completely. Why, no one knows.

It is a gradual, deliberately progressing infection wherein toes, fingers, nose, and jawbones are steadily gnawed away. It starts insidiously, and then affects either one or both systems, skin and nerves, yet rarely will by itself cause death.

Later I set out to find the Leprosarium. About half a mile from the mission hospital there is a small piece of land cut out of the jungle bush. It is no more than a square mile over all. The path leads on and on uphill and almost loses itself among the brush and high grass. It is not much worn. In the settlement many were working on clay bricks, cutting them out, drying them in the sun, and building walls. Rows of small adobe huts in crisscross lines were everywhere, built by the Lepers themselves. Each house is just large enough to accommodate a mother, father, and maybe a few or a flock of children.

One hesitates to enter one, as if Dante's inscription above the Gates of Hell were staring him in the face. *"Lasciate ogni speranza, voi ch'entrate!"*

There was hardly enough light to see. The floor was hard-packed clay and the windows too small to let in sunlight. There was a doorway, but no door. When my eyes got used to the darkness, I could see an old man shuffling slowly forward. He crossed both arms over his chest and where fingers and hands were supposed to be was a shapeless chunk, a round mass like boxing gloves. All his fingers had been lost in a painless, completely anesthetized way as through the years slowly one digit after another dropped off. The face, like a parchment with deep furrows, was a mask, unable to produce smile, express sorrow or emotion of any sort. It was hard not to recoil, even with medically trained mind and nerves. It was like being in hell and meeting men punished for crimes that could not be monstrous enough to merit suffering such as this.

I stepped back and outside; the flood of brilliant sunshine wiped out the ghastly image. Flowers in neat beds everywhere showed only too clearly that these people, too, love beauty, color, and all that Mother Nature can give them. Along every path cheerful little groups of pink, white, and red cosmos grew freely. Women, children, maybe broken in body but not in spirit, were everywhere, lovingly weeding and attending them. Flowers grew in profusion in front of their public meeting place, around the little schoolhouse, between their dwellings. People, many people, gazing and watching, tried to smile, but often it looked like a cynical sneer because of a distorted face. My fingernails were digging into the palms of my hands as I passed among them and looked into destroyed faces, some with black, gaping holes, some without noses and many with hands minus fingers and feet lacking toes. You have to watch them, talk to them, and live with them in order to see how they exist, and you become accustomed to this after you have stayed here a while.

You can get used to anything if you just try. . . .

A heavy-set, aged woman sat a slight distance away from me on the sun-baked clay ground. With patience that only an African native has she tried to select peanuts, picking them up with a hand having only two fingers left and pushing with the other having only a thumb, like a sore exclamation mark. Next she placed them into small mounds, watching carefully, by holding them together, that they did not roll away. What a heart-rending way to provide for a meal! Another joined in. She sat down and her feet were stretched flat on the ground; there was not a single toe left on either of them. One side of her face was gnawed away by this strange leprosy. Bone, muscles, skin were shrunken into a black hole.

Everyone was humble, cheerful, and hopeful here. How much one human can learn from another.

I examined many of them carefully. My curiosity allowed me no fear or realization of the danger of exposure. Principally what I saw here was the nodular type of leprosy. Consequently the chief manifestations were on the skin. The other known type, neural leprosy, was rare among them. Since I could not converse with them, the only way to recognize the involvement of the peripheral nervous system and with it the extensive anesthesia was to pinch or scratch feet, face, and skin surfaces of hands. Almost everyone had normal sensation to it. Many had gone blind because the leprosy literally gnawed the eyes out of their sockets.

Evening came and they lined up for their five drops of

chaulmoogra oil on a lump of sugar. It is bitter, burning, and is given to them as the only ray of hope. It is derived from the large fruit of a fibrous plant found in East India, Burma, and Ceylon. This oil arrests about 25 per cent of all cases and until recent years was the only form of treatment. Now, chemotherapy, Promin, and other similar sulpha preparations given by mouth, and streptomycin locally injected into the muscles, brighten the picture. Since 1941 these new preparations have been tried successfully and extensively in the United States and throughout the world. The result is encouraging.

This Dondi Mission leper colony! This Leprosarium, where inmates cultivate their own vegetable gardens, where they grow their fruit trees, maize, and peanuts, and where their chickens scratch under your feet.

I saw a small school there and in it one schoolteacher: a leper. I saw a little church there and heard service and singing, and in it a pastor: a leper. I saw many building houses and walls with skilled hands, if hands still remained: lepers. And I watched one sitting on the ground close to the small, trickling stream and working with fine skill to pattern grass mats: a leper.

All the days I was there I saw no one idling: all of them lepers.

Chapter VI

AT THE MUPA MISSION

W H E N I finally found the Catholic Mission at Mupa
late one afternoon, I was completely "bushed." Timetable
and logistics again went haywire. The truck behaved badly,
the gasoline-pump filter leaked because of corrosion from
the alcohol-containing gasoline. I lost my way and wandered
over anthills, wart-hog holes for many hours before locating
our direction.

This mission, a square with elongated whitewashed buildings around its perimeter, looked like an open-armed invitation. The buildings were porticoed with whitewashed clay
pillars, providing a shaded veranda across the front on its
full length. Everything around it was quiet at this late hour.
The fathers had retired. Here in this part of the world one
is sure that at any time and under any conditions one is
welcome!

The raucous tooting of the horn and flashing of headlights finally produced signs of life. The senior pater, with
keys jangling on a heavy chain around his white cassock,
greeted me with a kind face, smiling warmly in the light of
the candle he held. He spoke good English. Here I was,
arriving late and in pitch darkness, dog-tired. José had lost

his customary good humor and was anxious to find any place, even the top of a thornbush, to lie down and sleep at the first opportunity. The introduction was short and Pater Antonio's invitation was accepted quickly. He unlocked the door of the guesthouse. A simple, clean, whitewashed room with a straight, hand-made wooden bed, on it a tough straw mattress, and a pitcher and basin in the corner, looked good to my weary eyes. Everything draped with cobwebs silently proclaimed the dearth of guests. I was in it and underneath a coarse but warm blanket in no time, aware and appreciative of the enveloping comfort and serenity.

Morning came, as it always does. The tinkling sound of a little bell pealing cheerfully from the mission chapel and the chorus of youthful voices of black children evidently attending an early Mass woke me up. I lay in bed formulating plans for the days ahead. I was played out, the truck perhaps needed repair again, and in view of this sincere and warm hospitality I decided to stay here for a few days. I got up, dressed, and walked out in the sunlit square. These Catholic fathers rarely see white men in this forgotten bush country. They preach Christianity with one hand while holding the primitive plow with the other. They are poor in money and earthly goods, but infinitely rich in spirit, faith, and result.

Pater Antonio from Holland and Pater John from Germany met me as I walked toward the long, low-lying wing of their mission house. Just the two of them were carrying on here, both cheerful, efficient, and full of understanding philosophy. While the senior is the major-domo, the teacher, and the overseer of all property, the junior is the doctor and midwife, the lawyer and the spiritual help, as well as the wandering spirit among the primitives in this bush full of tribes all around the mission.

The natives are extremely interesting, I was told, and particularly for a doctor to see. Malaria, hookworm, bilharziasis, protein deficiencies, and many, many respiratory infections are especially prevalent. The good Father John, both doctor and priest, has to help even with the difficult labor cases, and they do exist here in abundance. By doing so, he explained, at least he is afforded a chance soon after to baptize them all as well. Experience has taught him to make keen observations and deductions. The new drugs such as penicillin and other allied antibiotics are available only in very limited quantity, so the small supply has to be spread thin and far. Many of the natives and particularly children are susceptible to all kinds of respiratory infections, pneumonias, as are the infants to whooping cough. They die quickly from it. The mycin drugs are truly a godsend, but so little is on hand. In his crudely carpentered medicine chest, as he opened its door held together with a string, were quinine and Atabrine for malaria, bismuth for all the diarrheas, and camphor as a stimulant. This miracle maker goes by oxcart into the bush often for days and weeks, answering the calls of the sick and needy everywhere. When he uses up his precious drugs, Epsom salts and aspirin are left as the universal medications.

For hours we talked and planned together and finally decided that as long as I was on hand, I would accompany him and use my own medical and surgical supplies to help. As he said, "Doctor, there are all kinds of fractures, many bad injuries, men and women mauled by lions; we need not go far. How long can you stay with us?"

"Well, we will see. I'll stay as long as I can be useful."

He chuckled. "Then you'd better stay here for good, Doctor!"

We headed for another building, which served as the dining room, where Pater Antonio was waiting for us. A huge, hand-carved, simple, sturdy table was at one end of the clay floor of a whitewashed and very clean room in which stood, of all things, an Electrolux icebox working on kerosene and the only one I have ever seen with a lock on it. "Trust your God and watch your neighbor." Now I understood the many keys on the long chain he wore. That vital piece of furniture and the food in it were worth guarding. After a short blessing the breakfast started in the usual lethargic African manner, giving us ample chance to eat, to meditate, and exchange views. In the middle of our contemplation, mastication, and conversation I heard a noise at the door. Pushing it open with its nose, a large gray horse came into the room and headed directly toward our table where Pater Antonio was sitting. He looked everything over slowly in a horsy fashion, snorting a little here and there and giving me an extra-lengthy gaze with a quizzical look in his watery brown eyes, making me feel rather uneasy and uncertain of his opinion of me. After he received his lump sugar from the table, evidently as part of his daily breakfast, he walked once around the room, clomping loudly and stopping in front of the Electrolux as though to make sure it was locked as all containers for valuables should be, and then ambled out into the sunny yard. No one else seemed to pay any particular attention to this disconcerting episode, so I, too, acted non-chalant.

A peaceful scene, like an oil painting by the early Dutch masters.

The paters got into a discussion of the relative value of methods of travel and the advantages of oxcart over auto-mobile. My recent experiences made me feel inclined to agree. After what I had been through lately, I was ready any time to exchange interrupted motorized horsepower for the more reliable and steady ox power.

The good Pater John with a twinkle in his eye explained that for years his best efforts on the natives often failed. While he preaches Christianity after delivering their women-folk and baptizes them left and right, the only result he gets is that they all seem delighted to wear on their neck the little cross he gives them—especially adorning themselves with it to go to their primitive dances. Lately it has become quite stylish among them to wear the little cross hanging down from one of their elongated ear lobes. They even go so far as to ask the good father for an extra one for the other ear lobe.

That is not so bad. In 1948 I saw a Masai early one morn-ing shivering with the cold, tie his enormously elongated ear lobes underneath his chin to keep his throat warm. So the fathers have yet to see a more spiritual application of their symbols.

Right after breakfast I climbed into an oxcart with him and had a firsthand lesson in this new form of travel. The seats were mats of straw, the kind that breaks the camel's back and had a similar effect on a different part of my anatomy. Progress was slow and devious, but obstinate like the nature of the beasts pulling us steadily ahead. It is curious how many small and large and decidedly hard obstacles can lie in the way of a pair of humpbacked oxen. After a few hours of this rugged and persistent endeavor to get somewhere I thought I would do better to "scramble out of this egg beater" and walk. While the good father with a long switch in his motionless hand dozed, his body swayed back and forth like a pendulum. The creaking of the enormous wheels, the cracking of the sides of the cart, led by a native holding the single pole attached between the two plodding beasts, blended in perfect harmony with this African setting.

Plowing through high, dry, yellow grass, leaving small patches of bush and cacti behind here and there, crossing countless sand-bottomed, dried-up creeks, we tumbled upon the village. Many women and more children, jet-black, naked save for a small loincloth secured with a bead-decorated string over the waist, were walking all around, busily husking corn, cleaning and collecting it into large calabashes and baskets, while the men were pyramiding the cornhusks close to the stockaded fence in several places. In the heat of the tropical noon sun young girls were breaking up corn with long wooden pestles, pounding mercilessly up and down on the kernels.

After making friends among them I started to film various scenes. Children were playing an interesting game. They formed a large circle, young and old alike, some hardly able to toddle and needing to be steadied almost constantly by older ones. They began to dance on the rhythm of the drum—*onoma*—and one child in the middle who was the lion—*ohosi*—rushed to catch one who then became the lion, a game similar to our tag.

I walked with the father to the different huts. Anxious faces, solemn supplication, and hopeful requests. Through a labyrinth of small alleys and openings we passed and came to the central part of the kraal. In front of the main hut, half sitting, half lying on the ground, was a very sick man, emaciated skin and bones, so weak that he hardly greeted us. "A man at death's door," I thought as I looked him over and realized that he was beyond my help. He was in the extreme stage of a crippling infection common to this part of the country which basically affects the urinary tract and is called "bilharziasis." It is a disease caused by one or two of three species of blood flukes or flatworms. Oddly enough, one species will attack and inhabit the veins only of the bladder and the interior parts of the genital organs. This is the *Schistosoma haematobium.* The other, also prevalent in other parts of Africa as well as in Angola, is the *Schistosoma mansoni.* The latter is more apt to infest the intestines and the liver. The female fluke is slender and looks like a thread under magnification. Because of her size she is able to wriggle easily through and into the narrowest veins. The remarkable thing about this fluke is its life cycle. After she lays her eggs, many of them pass with urine and feces out of the body, and get into fresh water. There they hatch out very quickly, in a matter of hours. Like hundreds of thousands of very fine filaments, they move in every direction and search, hunt, for their "host," the fresh-water snails. They attach themselves to the snails, penetrate their bodies, and there they grow into another form of maturity and in six weeks such larvae will swarm by the millions all around in the water.

Fresh water in the bush is indispensable for the natives. They swim in it, wade in it, wash in it, and they drink it. Once the native gets into such contaminated water, the larvae attach themselves to his skin and penetrate it, causing itching and only slight irritation of the skin.

They move back and forth through the network of the blood vessels, and quickly reach the minutest of them, and so are carried through the entire body. They feed on blood and lymph and grow into adulthood. They mate and migrate, and then lay their eggs again in the smallest blood vessels in and around the entire genitourinary system and often, too, in the liver, the heart, and the lungs. There they produce abscesses, fistulas, and a variety of other symptoms that often might lead to death.

What an amazing chain of events! As if they know just where to go, what to do and when to do it.

How can a primitive native, ignorant of all these complexities, protect himself from such calamity? How can he avoid fishing, wading, and crossing fluke-infested rivers, brooks, and pools? Malaria, sleeping sickness, bilharziasis, tapeworm, the results of protein deficiencies and many other killing and debilitating diseases, decimate his numbers.

What odds to live against!

And so this disease, too, saps life and strength slowly but surely away. There is an efficient medication, an injection therapy, available to cure or arrest this condition, but with the lack of facilities here for diagnosis and treatment what can be done for it in the bush? How utterly helpless must this good father feel and how much frustration is his share. Yet he keeps on trudging and trying time after time. I left some drugs to relieve the pain and tried to catch this dying man's eye and smile at him assuringly. Wives and children stood around while he lay motionless, stretched out on the sun-scorched, dusty ground, almost lifeless. Faith in fate and self-hypnosis wherein hope, comfort, and reassurance can be established are requisite. What can count more than that? We departed and I hoped that they would ask their diviner to take over where we left.

That same day before the sun set he died. No wailing, no crying, just acceptance of fate, and life went on.

" 'Now, come and tell me, Donisa, where has the lower part of your pants gone? What is it? Did you say something? Now, look here, little child, about two weeks ago I gave you a pair of blue denims. In the morning you arrived at our school with one leg of your trousers cut off below the knee. Next day you came and the other leg was missing. I told you that I am not giving you another pair of those jeans. After all, we don't have many. We receive them as gifts and we haven't received many of those lately. There are no stores here, no traders, and so we must be careful of the few we have. Now, Donisa, you are a little black girl child and though in the bush where you lived, you needed nothing but a G-string, here you have to wear trousers and trousers it must be, and I mean trousers with two legs on!' "

The good father of the mission went on telling me this story, homeward bound in the night.

"After a week passed I felt she needed another pair of jeans, so I hunted out the size to fit her and dressed her in them. She is clubfooted and the thin, spindly little left leg and foot, if covered, perhaps might make her feel better. She is a bright child, Doctor. We got her as an orphan. Her mother died in childbirth, as so many times happens. The father, heaven only knows where he is. He left the village and there she was, this four-year-old *oneñe*, and the relatives looking after her. Not much food to eat, crippled and lonesome. So here she is, with us. A name, of course, had to be given to her. The law requires it. Besides we, too, when baptizing her, had to select a name."

Pater John, while switching one of the oxen who decided to stop and rest, added with twinkling eyes, "You know, Doctor, it is hard for us two men, not too familiar with women, to find so many girls' names for so many orphans. This one we call 'Donisa.' "

"So what happened?" I asked.

"Oh yes. Donisa did get a second pair of jeans. We do not seem to recall exactly, but in a week or so we noticed that again both legs of the trousers below the knee were cut off, ending in a jagged, raveled edge. The matter had grown into quite a mystery and more or less of an exemplary situation, as well. Something had to be done. Donisa was cross-examined severely and questioned about it, but no explanation was forthcoming, just silence. The little girl with shiny, jet-black eyes, a thin little angular face, just stood there, now smiling, now serious, but without an answer. And so she was left alone. She played and walked all around like a gamin in the cut-off trousers, hobbling on the clubfoot. She was always there where her little bushy, curly-haired head just seemed to fit under your hand to pat whenever you happened to be reading the prayers or rosary. You know, Doctor.

"One day Donisa got ill. They are often sick, catching colds, infections, and what not, and only the good Lord knows how they hang on and survive. So often they get pneumonia and die. She was feverish and just lay on the cot. We have rooms for the orphan boys and rooms for the orphan girls. We always try to see that a few older boys or girls as helpers and companions are present. We know that when the sun sets they like to sing native songs, play games, native games just like they used to play in the bush, and so the older children playing with the younger ones make our supervision easier.

"Well, our little Donisa was sick and listless and I was worried, not knowing what to do. Fever was burning her up. We do have oranges; water we boil; and goat's milk is available. I left a gourd full of milk and a few oranges close to her cot, gave her quinine and some penicillin, and prayed to the Lord that my diagnosis was right and I would be helped through Him to save her."

Pater John's eyes were lowered and his hands rested on the side of the cart. He looked up at me as he continued the story.

"Now, Doctor, what do you think happened? After supper I sat reading in my room and Father Antonio was in his cell. I found my thoughts so much with the sick child that I could not go on reading, and went back just one more time to look in on her. The door squeaked loudly as I opened it and in the feeble candlelight among all the other sleeping children, there she lay, feverish and breathing heavily in slumber. What do you think I saw then, Doctor? Side by side on her cot, close to the thin little black hand, were four little dolls, dolls of exactly the color material of the missing parts of her jeans and trousers. Little woman dolls carrying little babies tied across their backs with thin strips of rag, little *totos*, that is all. It was a moving sight! I picked one up to examine it. There it was, a cob of kaffir corn used for the body, the face blackened with charcoal. You see, if we want to have a mother, if we need a mother, Doctor, we must have a black mother and so we must have a black baby, Doctor, don't you see?"

"Of course I see. We must have a charcoal-black mother and a little baby as well. How otherwise in this big, big wide world could little Donisas get along? Love is what we all need, isn't it, Father?"

And the oxen slowly pulling our creaking cart now to the left, now to the right under the starlit sky, just went on and on and on.

Chapter VII

THE MEDICINE MAN'S PRACTICE

I SPENT a few more days at the mission before starting south, and then went almost to the border of old German West Africa and turned at Pereira d'Eça slightly northwest, crossed the Cunene River with a pontoon at Forte Roçadas. The river is wide and flows leisurely here. Its shores are thickly grown over with papyrus and edged with treacherous swamps. This ferry was as unnerving and uncertain a vehicle as all the others I had been obliged to use in Angola. Crocodiles were floating like logs, looking at us with those vicious, staring eyes, and hippos bobbed up and down near shore. We made it to the other side, however, and soon ran into a primitive group of natives belonging to the Humbe tribe, who have settled in a village of the same name. They have undoubtedly the most picturesque hairdresses and combinations of colored beads in hair of the many I have seen in Africa. They wear two heavy flaps of hair matted together in saucer shape behind each ear and often fashion the hair in a ridge, like a Roman helmet going lengthwise of the skull down the center to the nape of the neck. They purchase these perukes, which are made of the clipped tresses collected when males or females cut their hair. The bands of brilliant yellow, red, blue, and white beads woven cleverly into the hair are strikingly decorative.

I had been on the go for days and now was getting low on food and had used almost all my water supply. At Pocolo I ran into one of those fantastic strokes of luck. I drove in with the truck and up to the *chefe do posto's* office and home, which was located high on a hill and under the shade of many eucalyptus trees. It was built of stone and cement with thick walls to keep the interior cool and low, overhanging roofs that shaded a veranda running entirely around it. The Portuguese Government sees to it that its officials get comfort and cheer, since they often have to remain at such outposts for years. I got out, stretching my legs as I walked up to meet him, never imagining the experience that awaited me. After the customary introduction and exchange of rather miserable French, English, and Portuguese to express our delight with each other, he, as they invariably will, offered his home, hospitality, and food. The food was good and the wine better. Drinking red wine is a favorite pastime with a Portuguese and he indulges this pleasure by taking wine in his coffee in the morning, in his soup at noon, and with hors d'oeuvres at night.

He was a bachelor with an avid interest in anthropology. He told me that his natives around here are secretive and hide their rituals and ceremonial dances. Nevertheless we could ferret out some information about a ritual dance that either had just been held or in the immediate future would be held not far from his post.

"There is a very picturesque and interesting primitive tribe which dances under the leadership of its medicine man whenever the bad or good spirits run amuck," he continued over another glass of wine. "If anyone is sick, some individual is always the cause of it. Natives do not accept natural causes for illness or death."

So the news had reached him through a "grapevine" literally or otherwise, referring to the large jug of wine in front of us on the table, that somewhere in the bush a dance was scheduled for the purpose of curing a "possessed" woman. We made a plan. The *sepaios* were then called in and lined up in front of us. Since they behaved as all native policemen do, either from rank failure to comprehend, or to avoid trouble for themselves by cleverly pretending not to understand, it took a great deal of ado and palavering to explain what we were after. One very old, weather-beaten character with funny-looking breeches cut off halfway and hanging loose on his spindly legs, wearing a safari jacket combination of uniform, finally came forward. Not a word of what transpired did I understand, of course, but I could discern a gleam in my friend's eyes, caused, I hoped, by the willingness of the sepaio to co-operate and not by the sudden appearance of a comely young native girl to clear food from the table.

Instruction was given to him to find out the details and for us there was nothing to do but wait. He departed and presumably made contact with one of the natives sitting around outside, or possibly he and another sepaio went directly to the village to find out when this dance would be held. I had to have patience. In Africa things move at snail's pace, so the very best thing my bachelor friend and I could do was to drink more Portuguese red wine, and this we did.

Just before noon the message came. The spirit-invoking dance would take place that very afternoon eight or ten miles south of the post in a wild, lonesome part of the bush. The word "bush" here qualifies an empty, sandy, desolate space with little vegetation. Sometimes years pass here without rain falling and the words "rainy reason" are rather inapplicable. The sparse, burned-up grass and low shrubs barely give any protection from the sun. Women and men are ebony black and only the thick pigment underneath the skin affords them shade.

The *chefe* and I got into cars; he in his small Austin pickup carried two sepaios and a few native girls belonging to the same village. I followed with my boy in the jeep. We soon got stuck. Quicksand held his Austin and I had to pull him out. That evoked roaring laughter from the natives. In the eye of the primitive the representative of law, order, and power should never fail. Dignity and respect were restored and we proceeded.

We stopped about a quarter of a mile away from a group of grass huts packed close together. As I approached the scene of the dance on that sun-scorched, yellowish clay ground, gazing at those black, glistening bodies and listening to the steady, deep tone of the drums, it was like a spell hanging heavy all around me. The medicine man, with one blind eye closed tight and drawn over with scarred eyelid, was naked except for a loose skin skirt. Around his waist he wore a braided skin forming a long tail on his buttocks. He looked like the very image of some sinister power emanating all the mystic influence of his trade. They paid little if any attention to me. I fumbled with my camera, getting it set, checking on lenses.

The moving bodies line up in a circle, leaving a small entrance place through which the medicine man enters into the center of that tense and already nearly hypnotized group of women. In an atmosphere of expectation silently and anxiously everyone is watching with eyes glued on him. As I grow more and more nervous, the air seems charged with electricity. It is noon, or shortly after. The sun relentlessly glares down almost vertically, no brush or trees around us. The few huts are deserted and not even dogs or chickens, which one usually sees around, are anywhere in evidence.

No men are in sight with the exception of the native witch doctor and myself with José. I know the *chefe*, who led my truck out here, must be somewhere in the vicinity, but where? Instantaneously as lightning a series of terrifying possibilities strikes me: What if this crowd gets out of control? What if it erupts beyond its boundaries? Where is the sick one? Where is the "possessed" woman? All these thoughts swarm in my head, yet beneath this apprehension lies a strong curiosity.

The drummers, three of them, one an exceedingly handsome, young, well-formed girl, another plump, with pleasantly smiling face, and the third like a gnarled old tree, are starting to beat the drums slowly with outstretched palms striking the skin tightly drawn over the oval-shaped wooden frames. They produce a rhythm and a distinct tonal difference, each drum harmonizing with the other. Like a weird cry of warning, it echoes dull and increasing in strength throughout the circle of women and the surrounding desolate-looking, lonesome huts. Bodies start to sway, intently following the motions of the man in the circle and he, with deliberate dancing steps, now forward and now backward, moves closer or farther away. The sound effect of the chanting and clapping hands, synchronized as if directed by an orchestra leader, melts into the deep and resonant sounds of the drums. Now one, now two of those gleaming, female bodies jump forward into the circle and dance in unison with the medicine man, with light steps crossing back and forth, merely to join the opposite side of the circle, where again they resume the chanting and hand-clapping as they disappear in the ranks of the others. The drums are beating faster, faster.

Then, just as I finish climbing, with the help of my boy, onto one flat-roofed, small, open stockaded hut to take different views and angle shots, I am suddenly aware that this entire circle, like an undulating mass of bodies swaying back and forth, is slowly and steadily edging toward two particular huts. One of them has in the center of its thatched roof a slightly bent, woven grass loop which evidently has an important connotation for them, the significance of which I do not understand. As the dance proceeds, here and there some of the participants stop while others keep on with it. Thirsty, heat-parched lips are gulping down water or native kaffir beer. The medicine man also takes a few long swallows. Strange, that with all this continuous dancing and bodily gyration he shows no signs of fatigue.

It could have been the heat or the mesmerizing effect of the continuous drumming and dancing that caused them all

And as far as the eye can see are the gently rolling hills, golden-yellow grass, and green palm trees.

"Contract labor"—a tr▮ load of natives off for mines.

Cunhama fishing. Men are in the front row; women with baskets just entering the stream.

Photo by De Sousa

Cunhama fishing. Waiting for the men to enter the stream.

Cunhama fishing. The conical-shaped form is made of reeds, with an opening close to the top for removing the fish.

Cunhama fishing. Cunhama women with their fishing baskets.

Cunhama wedding. The bride. Bridesmaids in background.

Photo by De Sousa

African cattle: four-legged legal tender of the native.

Cunhama wedding: giving fire to the elders.

Photo by De Sousa

The communal house of the leper colony.

Drying peanuts at the Dondi Leprosarium.

A leper's patience and endurance fill his life and peace is with him.

The strange disease of leprosy.

The old king, his wives, and bodyguard.

he first wife and the
ower behind the throne."

The chief and two of his wives at Gambos.

Photo by De Sousa

Colored beads, coins, headbands like jewelry, and manured coiffure are all part
of being "dressed up." Necklace and wide collar are characteristic of the tribes
of southern Angola.

Cooking. The triangular iron piece is used to slice squash in the basket.

Native mother with her children at Mupa.
Photo by De Sousa

One of the drummers, a native beauty of the bush.

The circle of participants. Diviner and sick woman are in the center. The hut i the right corner with grass loop on its thatched roof is where only the sick on is allowed to stay. *Photo by De Sous*

"Possessed" woman dance. The women drummers are starting the beat.

Excision ceremony: next year's candidates, 10 to 12 years of age. Feathers in air, tattooing on abdomen indicate tribal taboos and affiliation.

Beads in hair and many bark ringlets abov
ankle. Correctly attired, ready for pubert
rites.

Photo by De Sous

Entering puberty rites camp.
Sponsor stays with initiate
during months of training.

to view this fantastic scene through a hazy veil. My native colleague further increased the tempo of his already magic-like whirling.

A sudden weird cry, a shrill screech, splits the air as a tall, thin, almost ascetic-looking woman emerges from the hut distinguished by the grass loop on its roof. The entire circle of women and drummers, as if they are galvanized, react with more whirling and chanting and accelerated rhythm of clapping hands. The medicine man shakes his rattles con-stantly, close in front of and above the dancing, rigidly mov-ing women like a bird of prey follows its quarry, never let-ting it escape. Here or there another woman whirls out of line, dances across the circle, her black goatskin skirt flap-ping back and forth and on her ankles and arms metallic rings reflecting the brilliant sun.

At one time I am lying on the ground looking upward, then climbing onto any one of the hut roofs again, hardly conscious of what I am doing while shooting these scenes. My camera view finder seems too small to capture all this. Their mud-caked tresses hanging in rolls down to their shoul-ders, interwoven with yellow- and blue-colored beads, and the babies stolidly on their backs, shaken up and down, made this resemble a pagan scene of bygone centuries. Here I could feel that my modern training and medical, analytical mind completely failed. Here I, too, under the spell of this atavistic and brutal performance, realized fully the over-whelming power of mass hypnosis. Everyone joined for a single purpose here: to drive out the "bad spirit" from the "possessed" sick woman. It was a truly communal effort—all for one, all for the special benefit of one of the tribe. The sorcerer is no more than a catalytic agent; the fermentation follows its own inevitable pattern. What minute progress has modern medicine made toward the explanation of such scenes and effects! How perfectly simple this appears to the primitive and how hopelessly complicated to us! Our trained medical minds, strait-laced to the point where we tend to reject the things we cannot understand, erect a barrier that hinders our penetration into the cause of all this. Yet the result is here before me: this woman becomes more and more rigid, and the jerky movements slower and slower.

There is no more dancing now, only a steady drumming sound reverberates all around. The circle watches intently. Slowly, gradually a group of old women approaches the center. The sorcerer with his rattle precisely follows the movements of the sick as involuntary contractions and rapid jerks take over her face, shoulders, and arms.

Then her eyes roll, the white of her sclera clearly shows, the entire body stands rigidly as if frozen for seconds, and so with a shrill cry she falls forward. A dead silence clutches everyone. All the participants, staring and huddled together, follow the action of the sorcerer. They stand like helpless children engulfed in a storm of thunder and lightning brought upon themselves.

Suddenly the witch doctor with a piece of chalk—heaven knows how and from where gotten—makes a few marks on her legs and arms and a circle of white chalk on her forehead. There she lies, listless and limp on the ground while he mumbles and sings a weird incantation.

I forget all my filming and run to her. I check her: the pupils are wide, rigid, and dilated, the legs and arms are limp and no foaming at the mouth. What is it? Is it a true epileptic seizure, or is it a "Jacksonian" type of convulsion? My medical teaching, instinct for observation, and desire to help have come to the fore. A distinctly strange, silent, and unfriendly crowd watches me now and amid the unnerving hush I can feel the piercing look of the witch doctor upon me.

No, I shall not interfere! How could I, anyway? Do I know more about this than he? Certainly I could never produce this phenomenon, and decidedly not as deftly and smoothly as he did.

Congratulations, my colleague! Well done! With shaking knees I rose, picked up my camera, and left. The *chefe* emerged from somewhere and joined me.

All that night the usual remorse and doubts were with me again. Far in the bush the distant drums still throbbed. Would my films be all right? Did my hands shake too much? They certainly had reason to. Thus, with the drums sounding in my ears, and bodies whirling in front of my closed eyes, I fell into a heavy, nightmarish sleep.

The following day I left the area after bidding farewell to my bachelor friend at the post. While driving toward Sá da Bandeira my thoughts centered on the scene of the preceding day. What were the implications, the significance, the effect of the spirit dance I had witnessed in the bush? How much of the ritual was inherited, preserved through the centuries, and how much had been changed by the impact of the white man's civilization? Here in deepest Africa the uncivilized native is motivated or compelled by the age-old *mores* of his tribe to unite for the sole purpose, the Christian-

like purpose, of delivering help to a member who has been
singled out as needing it. The braided tail of the gnu (wildebeest), worn by the medicine man, and the magic rattles in
his hands are but visual manifestations of his sorcery. Beneath these superficial symbols lies a complexity of cause
and effect. Undoubtedly this woman will have many more
convulsions like the one I witnessed. My reasoning kept
questioning the cause of her illness. Her symptoms indicated
the type of epilepsy known as "Jacksonian," caused by direct
pressure on some part of the brain owing to a thickening of
either the membrane of the brain or an incorrectly healed
fracture of the skull. Such a condition can be caused by in-
jury at childbirth, or from a fall or a direct blow on the skull.
Therefore, I am sure that the convulsions I witnessed were
only a recurrence of past incidences of similar convulsions.
But how to account for the fact that this group of women
under the leadership of their medicine man was able, not
only to produce a spell sufficiently deep to bring this woman
out to join the dancers, but also to present at that specific
time one of those seizures? The deep-seated faith of those
natives who believe that by dancing and chanting and communal action they can temporarily, at least, expel the so-
called "bad spirit" from this woman demonstrates the
strength of their convictions. The village clearly recognizes
its responsibility toward one of its members whenever bad
or ancestral spirits lodge in one of its own. Why do those
spirits suddenly go berserk? The natives do not question.
They blindly and meekly accept the uncontested fact that
sometimes the sorcerer by employing "black magic" and
through sinister machinations will cast an evil spell upon a

member of the tribe. As a matter of fact, a man or woman will often come to him and pay him for doing just that. This custom puts him in an enviable position because then the one who received the bad effect of his spell must also come to him and pay him to undo the evil.

He does not inherit his status. Cunning ability to foretell events, or his inordinately well-developed power to psychoanalyze, raises him in the eyes of both men and women to a position that at first might be mere admiration and later evolves into a position of superiority. Then it is a foregone conclusion that he must prove his ability to maintain this exalted station by whatever clever means he can devise. This is accomplished by slyly and shrewdly applying his store of knowledge, surreptitiously gleaned from informers and unobserved study, to some particular problem involving one of the natives. He may have several understudies, some male or female accomplices in the tribe, who secretly relay to him information and details concerning feuds, differences, jealousy, hatred, or love between individuals or families, all of which he uses to advantage in the exploitation of his "calling." How convincing and successful he is and how aloof from the rest of the tribe he manages to remain depend entirely on his cleverness, his artful, scheming, and sometimes tactful approach to all his duties.

Whenever sickness visits a family or one of its members, or if difficulties arise in a hunt for game or locating a beehive, or for countless other reasons, they will consult him. Before the issue is settled, the native offers a sacrifice of a chicken, goat, sheep, or an ox, according to the importance of the matter. He, the medicine man, gets the lion's share of these sacrifices, since mortals are more in need of edibles than the spirits.

To me, as a white man and particularly as a physician, the native's unbelievable faith is remarkable. He is brought up from childhood with the understanding that the circumstances surrounding him and every episode in his life are arranged by good or bad spirits of his ancestors, or his enemies' or ill-wishers' ancestors whose wills are transposed into either persons or events affecting him. Thus the native, reared with undaunting trust in the medicine man, if he gets into any difficulty, goes in good faith directly to him, confident or at least hopeful that the sorcerer one way or other will alter the intentions of the spirits, and believes that he alone has the power to do it. To the medicine man he attributes superhuman qualities. The simple native therefore is a remarkable subject for this form of sorcery. Every phase of the medicine man's practice, from influencing his subjects by elementary psychology to producing this amazing spectacle of the spirit dance, is obviously prearranged.

The most vital and equalizing factor in this setup is that the sorcerer himself cannot abuse the power bestowed on him. If he is using it for the benefit of the entire tribe and his decisions appear justifiable in the opinion of the majority, the system functions smoothly. By utilizing his power and influence to stabilize the evil in one or several individuals by cleverly intimating selfishness, greed, or petty thievery, so that the person involved gets more or less conscience-stricken, he is able to keep the village together as a closely knit organization, and under the beneficial, restraining effect of the elders of the tribe he can guide and practically create public opinion. However, if he should take a willful and incorrect attitude frequently enough, this simple faith would weaken and, once shaken, his almost hypnotic influence would weaken simultaneously.

How remarkably well balanced such a society is.

The white man must go slowly in imposing his laws arbitrarily on the native and expecting him to live by a standard of punishment made to suit the crime. As yet incapable of understanding such laws, naturally he is lost and confused. If he leaves his tribal area beyond the control accepted as his natural law, the result is that he falls into economic difficulties, becomes easy prey of prostitution, and learns how to steal and lie. It is readily seen that if this balance is disturbed either by overzealous efforts of missionaries forcing an alien religious belief too quickly on the native, or by applying the white man's laws to him through traders and the like without a slow and careful approach, a vacuum can easily be created. Then, without actually being "detribalized," this well-integrated community will lose its own ability to decide right from wrong and to feel the consequences of their deeds. Such a community is from thereon bereft of effective means of meting out good for the good deed and bad for the bad.

Under these conditions isn't it hard to offer the native something better as a substitute for what is taken away from him?

Chapter VIII

MUTILATION OF YOUNG GIRLS

A BLANK FACE was the perpetual response to my inquiries about secret and painful operations on native girls at the age of puberty. In Luanda I broached the subject in order to learn where such an operation might still be practiced, or, if it was practiced in the past, to hear some of its methods. My good Portuguese friends just laughed and told me to forget it. "It just does not exist any more."

Again in Nova Lisboa I brought the question up, hoping that, being closer to the uncivilized tribes in the area, I might find out something about it. The answer was "Nonsense! It is not practiced any more. Besides, the government, itself, would stop it anyway."

My medical colleagues there often talked about health problems, the diagnosis and treatment of tropical diseases, and I spent many hours with several well versed in medicine and its allied problems. So I asked if they could help me. Not one of them knew or wanted to admit a thing about those practices. I ran into one Swedish missionary doctor who mentioned that he delivered native women in very difficult labor owing to mutilation-ritual operations carried out on them in their youth. But he did not know from whence they came and to what tribe they belonged.

"They are here now and there tomorrow," he said. "Some might drift in from the south or west, while others might never come close to civilization. If any of the mission staff runs into the aftereffects of such mutilation, it is impossible to track down its origin."

As a matter of fact, while I visited the mission at Dondi, Dr. Gilchrist also mentioned cases he happened to see with mutilations on the clitoris, or on the small labia, presenting difficulties later in labor owing to the extensive scar tissue formation.

"But they all come from the south," he explained to me. "The Ovimbundu of central Angola is so substantially civilized that, in having abandoned many of its original and age-old native rituals, most, and certainly such excision puberty rites ceremonies, are completely forgotten." So he could not help either.

It was up to me to do my own "digging" and constant questioning to find a lead. The farther south I drove, the more noticeable was the change in behavior, dress, hair-do, and life of the native. The central south, a few hundred kilometers from the Benguela-Lobito Railway, which bisects Angola, is a vastly different country from the north and northwest especially. The tribes here are cattle breeders and many of them are still totally nomadic. Contact with the white is rare and the vast stretches of high tableland are sandy and bush-covered. The large forest areas with small trees make contrast with the north more emphatic. Between the Cunene and Cubango rivers south of Vila da Ponte and Serpa Pinto,

Africa stares into your face as one will seldom find elsewhere. The game roaming in the bush, herds of elephant, man-eating lions and leopards, the roan antelope in small or large groups, galloping on the dry grassland are a fitting background for the primitives here.

I had followed the Cunene for days, keeping my direction almost due south. The region was thickly wooded, the bush full of elephants, and every night one could hear the trumpeting, stampeding herds drawing down to the river for drinks and baths with their young ones. There is nothing more noisy than an elephant nursery watched over by anxious cows. All night I heard their tramping and screeches of their little ones, accented now and then by the roar of a lion. I kept my night camp as far as I could away from the river's shores; the bugs and mosquitoes were less likely to be troublesome a bit farther inland.

Into Capelongo, a dot on the map and the home of exactly two white traders, right in the heart of south-central Angola I drove my maimed jeep late in the forenoon. It happened that, a few days before, we had hit a fallen log and then smacked into a wart hog's hole, comical enough for his family but not much appreciated by me, and had broken a leaf in the right front spring, and we had to go slowly from there on. We tied a strong sapling to it and it helped sufficiently so that, limping, groaning, and creaking, we were able to proceed in a gingerly way.

We arrived at the *chefe do posto's* station. The *chefe* had troubles. His ulcer bothered him and he had returned to his post but a few days previous, after all kinds of medical checkups but no help from the only civilized source about a hundred kilometers away. If a man has stomach ulcers, it is likely caused by his disposition—and a not too pleasant disposition—and when a man goes out of the bush for days of hard traveling to get relief for his ulcer and then comes back because no help was found, his disposition is certainly not apt to improve. He looked as sore as a boil. My best effort and all my advice could produce from him nothing better than a lukewarm smile. At any rate the chefe was sick, the broken spring needed repairing, and the country was wild. After he stated, though with not much enthusiasm, that there was a Portuguese close to his post who could forge a new spring leaf for us, I decided to stay, influenced more by fatalism than by his invitation.

The few natives standing around and watching us stolidly impressed me as being ready to cook me in a pot and eat me soon after.

We started to unpack and get ready to cook a meal. Much to my surprise a sepaio brought an invitation from his boss to come over and dine with him. Well, this was unexpected—the first step toward "defrosting." Often those officials do not have much to offer in the way of food, but they generously share it with you always. Canned fruits and vegetables are delicacies and they see such things only by looking at the advertisements in *The Saturday Evening Post*. Incidentally, the only American magazine they had there was *The Saturday Evening Post*. So I got together some jerked meat and a couple of cans of Del Monte's mixed fruits, coffee powder, and canned milk, and ambled over to his house. When we got warmed up and I got into my own element, I gave him several pointers on how to live with his ulcer—if he wanted to have other people living with him—then filled him up with two raw eggs he had on hand and some atropine tablets I had on hand. That did the trick. His pain disappeared soon afterward and a big, broad smile was the visible result. He joined me for some boiled rice and canned fruit and by that time he became so internationally minded that I could easily have induced him to join the United Nations.

I asked the chefe whether he knew anything about excision puberty rites ceremonies among the people in his vicinity. He of course said, "No." That by now did not surprise me at all. But in the next breath to my astonishment he continued, "But if you, Senhor Doctor, are really interested and want to be convinced, let us ask my sepaios. They are all from the tribe of this area and if any puberty rites are practiced here, with or without mutilation, they will know about them."

So we went to his office, situated opposite his house, where several of his native police boys were waiting. What more could I ask?

We entered his office and got the boys lined up. Four of them, all highly suspicious and dubiously bright characters, stood at attention. I had to work by process of elimination and since my words had to be translated, not only from English into Portuguese so my friend with the ulcer could understand, but from Portuguese into the native tongue, time was needed and patience galore. José, alert as always like a dog on a scent, watched my eyes and acted as though he felt equally responsible for my success or failure. My good friend Antonio de Soŭsa whom I had had with me since Nova Lisboa, worked like a court translator in some city magistrate's office trying to translate and transform at the same time. The chefe was belching at regular intervals, visibly improving after each such eruption, and concentrating on the scene with an ever-increasing interest.

Three of the four were quickly ruled out. They were so positive with their answers and so emphatic with their lies and denials that I knew it was no use to probe them further. But the fourth, the fourth, he had something about him. It challenged me and appeared to be worth the time and trouble to spend an afternoon cross-examining him. This old wizard with a smile that looked as if someone with invisible wires were simultaneously pulling his mouth sidewise, nose upward, and eyes crosswise, looked like promising material. To begin with, he never answered any question promptly and directly. He would shift his weight from one foot to the other, at times standing in stork fashion on one foot only, with the other leg bent and its foot resting against the knee of the straight, stiff leg that supported him. He acted as though he knew plenty and had decided to keep us from knowing anything. We kept on asking questions, all kinds, leading and seemingly innocent, important and irrelevant, but his answers were evasive and concealing.

"Do you know if any dance will be held in the bush?"

"*Sim, senhor,* there will be."

"Do you know the reason why the dance will be held?"

The wire-pulling went on and the mouth was up, the nose down.

"*Sim, senhor,* because the people want to dance." (*Humph!* Good answer.)

"Why do the people want to dance just now?" and here the shifting of weight from foot to foot took place again.

"I don't know, senhor." (All right, let's start another way.)

"When will the dance be?"

"Tomorrow, senhor."

"When tomorrow? In the morning, afternoon, or night?"

"In the morning, senhor." (Maybe now I have a clue! The native does not dance in the morning and seldom in the afternoon, but almost always after sunset. I will get you now, you old devil! There must be some special reason to have a celebration of such extraordinary importance for a dance in the morning, so let's see if we can corner you.)

"Did you say the people will dance tomorrow morning?" (Now the old fox senses something. He is getting close to a trap.)

The smile came on again, a little extra shifting, a bit more hesitation, eyes moved back and forth, lowering, raising, and piercing me during the slight wait, and yet behind them a studied and definite intention not to give himself away.

"I don't know if they will dance in the morning."

"But you must have known when you left the village today. Didn't you talk to the men this morning before you came to the office of the chefe? Now come, come."

All this in quick succession, yet consuming much time, is translated from English to Portuguese, from Portuguese to his language. José is working, my friend is working, and the *chefe* is watching.

"*Sim, senhor*, perhaps they will dance tomorrow morning."

"Then why will the people dance tomorrow morning? You

know your people seldom dance in daylight. Come on, now, tell us the truth."

By now the chefe was becoming so interested that between belches he began bellowing in exasperation at his parrying subordinate.

Something is being concealed here, it was obvious, and it must be something very worth while to merit this persistent effort to cover it. There was an hour or more of verbal pulling and tugging, cross-examining and questioning, answering and translating, belching and arguing. Finally the old sepaio confessed that about four or five kilometers distant there is a camp, a camp which has been built for some rites involving young girls and "it just happens" that the folks around will dance there, and "it just happens" that they will dance there in the morning. Then I made a careless slip: I asked him point-blank if he knew anything about any operation or ceremonial excision on the girls. A stone silence followed. There he was, frozen up; he would admit nothing.

"*Não, senhor*, there are no sick girls at the camp. No, *senhor*, I don't know what operations and what rites you talk about. *Não, senhor*, I never saw or heard about any mutilation of young girls in our tribe. *Não. Não. Não, senhor*."

Being so direct was my mistake. I should have felt my way and pieced together my own conclusions. Now this sly old wise fellow was on guard and when a native is on guard, he just shuts up. At least I was on the track and wouldn't think of giving up now. So I started again in a somewhat different way, intent on catching him off guard.

"Where is this camp, sepaio?"

"What camp, senhor?"

"The camp you talked about where the dance will be held tomorrow morning."

"Oh, senhor, it is in the bush and I really don't know how to find it, senhor."

"Oh yes, you can, and you *will!*" bellowed my ulcer case. "This morning you just came from there. You are one of them, you surely know where they are and where the dance will be held."

I realized that the prodigious power of the law comes in handy at times and consequently I chose this moment to retreat, leaving the official and his sepaio alone, not to exchange their views, but to have a one-sided explanation. When I returned, alterations were visible. The wires that worked the sepaio's smile were evidently crossed now and his right eye being closed, it was difficult to know in what direction he was looking. At the same time my co-operative friend, the chefe, though still belching occasionally, did not need to bellow again. My raw-egg treatment had paid off, and now the sepaio had cause for one of a piece of raw steak.

This time the conversation resumed with noticeably more willingness on his part. He suddenly remembers the place and will take us there in the morning on our request. That was enough. It looked as if by sheer luck I had unearthed a camp for girls in the midst of puberty rites ceremonies. I did not know if they were actually operated on, where the camp was, how long it was in use, or if I would be allowed to see anything in it, but at least I had a lead.

The chefe was now curious too. He did not even dream that something like this could go on near to his post, had never heard of it, and would never have believed it. I suggested that he keep the reticent sepaio under lock until morning so no news would get to the camp, and that it might be wise to keep our eyes on the other three boys as well. If one went into the bush to warn them about our coming the next morning, they might pull stakes and leave. They could easily send the girls into the bush to hide and on our arrival the whole picture would be changed. Therefore, it was agreed that there would be nothing safer than to have his entire police force behind bars for the night.

The chefe was now decidedly more cheerful and sociable owing to the cooked rice and raw eggs and a little bicarbonate of soda. He became talkative and explained that the tribes around Capelongo for the most part belong to the group of Quipungos, Humpata-Huilas, and Gambos. They are primitive in varying degrees. The operation on the girls, if done at all, surely is done so secretly and kept from the eye and knowledge of the white so well that it could seldom be witnessed. I wondered what concoction they use to dope the candidates, what dances they perform, and who does this "excision," or "incision," or "defloration." Formerly an actual mutilation was carried out, but lately most of the tribes have gotten away from that and use either a blunt instrument or polished end of a small horn to carry out the "defloration," which is a slow and daily-repeated, painful process, breaking through the hymenal ring and dilating the vaginal entrance in preparation for intercourse. It is always done by an old woman and she is either a member of the same tribe or sometimes borrowed from another.

Among some tribes the "incision" is a slit cut made with

either a sharp mussel shell or glass between the small and large labias. Those south of here roaming the northern border of South West Africa use a triangular-shaped, sharp piece of iron hammered out and fashioned with a short iron handle to remove a part of the small labia. This is the "excision," a mutilation operation fraught with danger. The bleeding can be not only severe, but at times uncontrollable, although they do often use an astringent fluid, boiled up leaves, roots and barks of certain trees and shrubs, and wood ash, too, the last being particularly successful to control bleeding as well as infection. However, infection often follows and many of the girls are sick sometimes for weeks and months, and carry the mark of this rite as a large and extensive scar formation.

I went to bed with head buzzing and full of questions. Walking across to the truck, I needed no light. The full moon poured its silvery-white rays like a milk bath over the whole countryside and only the snoring of José, stretched out under the truck, brought me back to stark reality.

Next morning amid chattering of many birds and monkeys we all got ready. Our prisoners were released from the mud-plastered jail and if they had any plan to mislead or divert us, they cloaked it well this time behind pleasant and smiling faces.

We started. I sat the old wizard on the right front fender and one of his assistants on the left. Just to be sure that if one disappeared I would still have others as hostages, two more climbed up in the back of the truck. The chefe was not anxious to come along and explained, full of apology, that he felt worse again. It didn't matter, since I knew I would have to carry the burden of decision and action from here on anyway. The fewer white people present, the better would be my chance. The old fox on the fender pointed to the right or left as we bounced along, indicating which way to turn in the high grass and thickly wooded bush country.

Shortly he signaled to stop, and then we proceeded on foot with cameras, films, cigarettes, and a large carafe of wine. We trudged a few kilometers on the hard-baked, dusty ground, getting full of prickly thorns and itchy grass, making me scratch all over, when suddenly a wide clearance opened up. Trees here in the south are not too large. The bush is dense and the average growth is three to four feet. Here was a stockaded, small-sized village. Barking dogs with a few elder males walked out to greet us. One, bent with age, leaning heavily on a small stick, came forward directly to meet me and a conference started. I, as usual, took a lively part in the palavering, gesticulating and grimacing, smiling, but not understanding a word. Again with José's help the routine worked well. He gave out a handful of cigarettes and usurped the conversation, shrewdly blocking the foxy old sepaio from getting in a word. I kept the three other chums of his in the background with a meaningful, determined glare to show that if one wrong word were dropped, they would be mutilated too. The preliminaries worked. There was much smiling and handshaking now.

Another very old man came forth, his head finely sculptured as if chiseled out of ebony, and his eyes warm, kind, and intelligent. He looked me over as if he had to make the final decision. To this one I offered the wine. He accepted it, drank with a great deal of dignity and gave it over from mouth to mouth in a row. Eyes were rolling and protruding Adam's apples moved up and down while the divine nectar was gulped, and then a serious conference started. A few old women shyly joined them as they stood around. I asked José to tell the sepaio to explain that I, as a medicine man for the white, came from a faraway country and because I knew that they had some medicine they concocted and used to drink here to make people go to sleep, I wanted to witness how it was done. "Is it true?"

There was silence and hesitation.

"José, you make this old rat," and I was pointing toward the sepaio, "tell to the *sekulus* [elders] that I know definitely that it is so, and there is no chance to evade the answer, and that I know by talking to this sepaio," pointing to my by now day-old acquaintance, "that they have girls right here who a few days ago were given such drinks."

At this point I was careful not to refer to the reason why they should be given such drinks, or that I could have any inkling of any mutilation.

With José's help I continued. "I, too, have some powerful medicine with me and with it I can stop pain instantly. I can make one's bellyache disappear." This moment I regretted that the chefe had not come along to prove it. I wanted to stay around the village for the day. I stated that I would do no harm and came only to learn what they did and compare whether or not they did it better than what I could do. There was more talk among themselves and hesitation before the wily old sepaio came to the rescue. It looked as if he were not as bad an egg as I had thought him the day before. I don't know what he told them, but it was evident the moment he stopped his gesticulation and pantomime that something was decided—and in my favor!

The few women standing around began to cry out loudly a sort of weird signal and this was answered back from the village. Now it was time to give more cigarettes and wine. That was accepted and I, too, was accepted. The *sekulus* lined up with me and headed toward the entrance. Under the small elevated logs blocking the narrow entrance way I stopped and stooped to pass. Once inside I immediately started filming. I did this to demonstrate that while I kept moving my camera in all directions, running it and rewinding it, nothing extraordinary would happen to them. A timid lot, unpredictable, they had to be reassured, and being nonchalant, paying little attention to them, served my purpose well.

Inside the encirclement several women and younger girls were brewing a drink of some kind in large calabashes and iron pots. The beer—*mbamvu*—as usual was a maize and manioc mixture probably fermented for days before and was not yet ready to use. There was much activity and a good deal of walking back and forth.

Two young girls, ages ten to twelve, emerged from one of the huts and a man with a drum joined them. I stood back and watched. Both girls were decorated with ostrich feathers on their heads and beads hanging down both sides of their hips. They wore earrings and delicate, lovely necklaces. One had tattoo marks on her chest and abdomen, but the other was entirely free of them. One was darker and more characteristically Negroid than the other, who had a yellowish velvety sheen to her skin and Caucasian features. Here and there between the huts other girls of the same age group, with white, blue, and red glass beads woven into their hair, were watching intently, peeking around corners. Many had numerous ankle bracelets made of tree bark on both their legs reaching almost to the knee. Their yellow-brown bodies and butter-smeared shoulders and necks glistened in the sun. Those were the candidates for next year's puberty rites initiation, as I found out later.

And then the dance started with the drum music. At first just little tapping movements of the feet as the two youngsters in the middle, singing the same tune, upper bodies moving and swaying, formed the core of the entire scene. Their comrades commenced to leapfrog around them and soon the group was electrified. Young women joining them with bent knees, some with babies on their backs, danced around. More drummers were added, and then as the circle slowly took shape, the older women stood around only looking on and clapping hands.

An albino woman led a strange procession out of one of the huts. A horrid sight she was, the very incarnation of homeliness, pink eyes, sore and swollen eyelids, the inflamed-looking, raw white skin of her face, the Negroid full lips, the small, sore, excoriated sections along arms and hands that, because of the lack of pigmentation, left her body unprotected from the sun's strength. She bore this apparently without much discomfort and undoubtedly was the principal female sorcerer, *Nyambutsi*—Mistress of the Rite—the much-needed personage here. Often at such camps as this an albino is a necessary fixture. The reason behind it no one seemed to know. She perhaps personifies some form of strange spirit. If such an individual is not available, villages go to the extent of borrowing one and paying heavily for her services with oxen, sheep, or goats.

In a single line several native women followed her, one leading a young girl who was completely befogged. The last, holding with both hands onto the shoulders of the woman in front and walking rigidly, slowly, with face down, was evidently under the effect of a drug. Another woman with another girl in the same condition closed the line. They made their way slowly to the dancing circle and stood watching silently.

The dancers were singing loudly by now, the drums were beating heavier, and not one of the dancing groups noticed this curious procession. The girls stopped leapfrogging and two men, like enormous birds bending and swaying toward each other, started to dance while the young, heavily drugged victims, like senseless humans, seemed neither to hear nor see what was going on. Occasionally a young girl attendant of the initiated with solicitous attention wiped away their freely flowing nasal discharge with a small piece of wood. Wide open eyes revealed dilated pupils, rigid and not focusing at all, like a cataleptic; both stared at the ground. On one's face a fly landed and not a muscle twitched, indicating lack of sensation. Both had their hair tightly braided over the temples and a few bead decorations. They looked well developed with signs of sexual maturity.

The albino watched them like a hawk, and me as well. I sensed that she was not particularly pleased with my presence and certainly not with my movie camera. The dance kept on, it was close to noon, the sun was fierce.

The two young females were under the effect of heavy drugging and evidently still in pain, though their facial expressions would not indicate it; yet, though they walked slowly, they walked with effort. There I was, witnessing what I had been told did not exist. These two girls must have had something done to them beyond any doubt—and recently.

If only I can sneak into that hut from which they came, it might be that others are still there. Gradually, feigning interest in the dogs, huts, a few chickens, and roaming children who, just like the grownups, are swaying to the drum rhythm and clapping their little hands, I edge toward the hut. It is a square rather than round type of structure, with an unusual flat roof. The walls are not stockaded sticks, but high, dried-out stalks of kaffir corn, and instead of a narrow, low opening with planks above, as is customary, the entrance is fairly wide, high, and square.

I had one eye on the albino. She is watching her victims intently now and all the women are occupied with the dance, most of them in a closely crowded circle with the few men inside.

I reach the hut and peek in. Sure enough, there are two more girls huddled together lying on the ground and covered with rugs. I must see. I don't care if they get angry, if they explode. They might harm me. I left my guns behind—no protection—but José is here, the sepaios are too, and even if they do not agree, they are the authorities in the eye of the primitive here, and the agents of the law. Now I am bending on my knees to look at their eyes. Let me see. Confound the darkness in here! These eyes are closed, the lids are rigid, but when opened the pupils are wide, dilated, exactly like the victims outside. A smell on the breath? Can I detect what they have been given? My head close to their bodies, I notice a heavy, deep, unconscious breathing almost like that produced by narcotics. Their limbs are limp. I look back over my shoulder. No one is at the entrance. The steady drumming, singing, and chanting go on. I lift the edge of the rug and throw it back. A dirty piece of linen covered with ash is wrapped around both upper thighs holding them closely together. It is blood-soaked. Close by on the ground is a small horn, like the horn of a reedbuck. The girls have been deflorated.

Pandemonium breaks loose! I hear the old witch yelling and the dance breaks up. The drums stop.

She is in the entrance now, she has caught me in the act. I get up and leave the hut with a calm expression, walking past her into the brilliant sun as if nothing had happened. Then, with a forced equanimity, I point my camera toward this troublemaker. I could well choke her at this moment. She in turn, so taken aback with my aplomb, stands still and mutters.

The drums start once more. The little girls with ostrich feathers are swaying as before; the albino looks uncertain as I smilingly join my group. While I watch what will happen next, my thoughts are back in the hut where those girls in bloody rags lie in the ash.

The dance goes on and on. Beer is offered to me and I must accept it. I lift the gourd and go through the motions. Is it possible that the commotion is forgotten, or is there pretense of ignoring it? Where is that old chaperon now?

Nowhere can I see her. She must be in the hut where those "prizes" of hers can be more securely guarded.

I am thirsty, hungry, and tired. The crowd grows, more men and women arrive, and now the dance is under way. Slowly as it came, goes the strange line, albino leading the "sponsors" and the two girls back to the hut to join their comrades. No doubt there will be more rites and ceremonies. I must take care to stay on their good side, to assure them that what I saw I accept without criticism. I must convey to them that I want to stay around for a while and I must be accepted without fear when I return next day.

Chapter IX

THE WHIPPING

I TURNED to José and asked him to tell them that it pleased me to see their dances and if I should come back another day, I might bring more cigarettes, wine, and some salt to them. Among this simple and rather suspicious band in important moments it is better to convey an impression of uncertainty and hesitation instead of outright promise, thus keeping them tense and in an expectant mood.

As I started to leave, heading toward the truck, a *sekulu*, one of the elders, came haltingly forward. He had a request, so I stopped and waited until he collected courage enough finally to show me his sore eyes, silently pointing toward them and blinking heavily. They were inflamed, matted together owing to a purulent discharge, and no doubt infected. Eye infection, and often trachoma as well, is prevalent among the natives of Africa. The ever-present flies, carrying all kinds of germs, attach themselves to the eyelids in rows. It seemed as if each man, woman, and child had his own allotted number of flies carried on him constantly. It is a revolting sight.

So here was an added opportunity to win good will. Now that one asked for help, the others would follow. I would

be welcomed back the next day with my medications, oint-
ments, eyedrops, dressings. José sensed the crucial moment
and was quick to exploit it to the utmost. Immediately taking
over the conversation amid much pomp and circumstance,
he repeated that I would return next day and treat all who
needed help. Thereupon we left.

While driving to the post, the old rascal I had so much
trouble cross-examining before now readily and sponta-
neously disclosed, contorting his mobile face and mimicking,
that soon another kind of dance plus ceremony with some
form of whipping would take place, directly connected with
the puberty rites. José told me this; I could not understand
what he was talking about, but it was repeated again and
again. I was assured that there would be a dance or ceremony
in which men and women flog each other with sisal whips and
it would be held in the same village.

That night I pondered and searched for an explanation,
attempting to integrate into a comprehensible picture all I
had witnessed. How were those girls operated on and how
many days ago? Was the operation an incision, was it an
excision or only defloration? Who performed it? What were
the rules requiring the presence of the albino? Who was that
old witch who interfered? What did those girls drink? How
often after the operation were they given such drinks? That
the ones I saw being led out holding onto the shoulders of
their "sponsors" were definitely under the effect of some
drug was evident. Yet how about the ones in the hut? The
ones lying on the ground moaning and not yet fully conscious? Why were they still drugged and doped? Perhaps in
addition to the soporose effect of those drinks the girl candi-

dates had been exposed to constant day- and night-long chanting and drum playing before the horrid, bloody ritual and were spellbound, mesmerized sufficiently to endure it without a sign of pain. The presence of the albino was no doubt significant. She was the personification of magic power. Whatever the case may be, here at the middle of the twentieth century this tribe still employs weird persons for weirder magical purposes.

The next morning I did not go back. I got information that the dance would be held the following day in connection with the sisal-whip ceremony. I felt that my presence there might disturb their routine and perhaps even precipitate a change in their plans and dances. But the day was spent usefully. For hours I tried to work more on the old sepaio. We no longer had to lock up the others—they liked the lodgings so well that they went to the jail to sleep from choice. After my cooking and dishwashing that morning I sent José for him. He arrived dirty as a stovepipe, showing on his wrinkled face the anticipation that more cigarettes and wine might be his share and happy that we were on speaking terms again.

"Now, tell me, when will the whipping and dance be held?"

"The day after the sun goes down, *senhor*."

"Do you think that you can take me there?"

"*Sim, senhor*, I will be glad to do so." Of course by now he was glad to do anything; cigarettes, wine, and money were obviously on his mind.

"All right, then, we shall go there tomorrow."

José was extremely pleased. He catapulted himself to a

height, in the eyes of the sepaios, where no doubt they thought that he and not I was the one who decides what to do, to see or not to see. Carrying my cameras, handling films under the unmistakable admiration of those natives, being a part of opening and closing that mysterious black box, and creating the impression that without him I could neither manipulate nor continue to work the cameras made him exceedingly proud. His gesticulations became more succinct and expressive, his sentences had an authoritative ring, and his gait and countenance took on a decidedly distant air. To top it all, he changed attire and fished out from the depths of his bundle a worn army cap, replacing his white sun helmet, and demonstrated his efficiency more than one way during those days. He not only washed and dried my coffee-pot, but polished it with sand so extensively that for several days I ground particles of it between my teeth. In fact he went so far as to take my razor apart to put a sharp edge on the blade with a piece of stone. The result of that rough treatment was that I could not shave until I replaced it with a new one. He insisted on washing my shirt according to the proven native fashion, taking it down to the nearby creek, pounding it while wet, and swinging it against a slab of stone so that every single button broke off of it. Yet in all this José meant well, and I would rather have worn the shirt without buttons than the shirt with buttons but without him.

Most of the day was spent in inconsequential activity around the camp, at times wondering whether or not the *chefe* was better or worse. This I did not find out till the late afternoon when we got together for a cup of tea. He was my guest this time and, sitting under the canvas lean-to attached to the rear of the truck, in royal fashion elevating his legs on one of those army chairs, he belched but twice.

And so I returned to the village. Long before arriving I could hear weird, shrill cries and a great deal of commotion. The gnomelike face of my leader smilingly looked back at me, and he behaved like the sole impresario of an operatic production just about ready to unfold. José, too, grew restless, fiddling with anything he could put his hand on and stuffing his army-coat pockets with film magazines for all eventualities. It amazed me how well this simple boy with no training or education in the formal sense could intuitively know what was expected of him. It was remarkable how well he could anticipate problems or wishes and how quickly he did adapt himself to them and be useful to the maximum under such conditions. It might be because his brain power and reasoning, uncluttered by many of modern man's do's and don't's, can work more to the point as a simplified yet efficient mechanism. For instance, he even warned me, pointing at the turret of the Bolex, not to forget to remove the dust cap on the lenses, as I so often was apt to do. He listened to the humming of my camera motor to detect trouble and time and time again I noticed him critically looking up toward the sky with half-closed eyes just to judge the strength of light, as he had so often seen me do, as though he knew the significance of a light reading and to what extent light values affect the film. They are great actors and imitators.

We arrived.

On the open, dry clay ground, fenced in but not a part of the village, were two lines of people facing each other.

In the midst of shrill voices like those of distraught, chattering parrots a dozen sturdy males stood with backs against the stockaded fence, holding in both hands good-sized straight sticks three to four feet in length. Opposite them was a line of young females some of whom had multicolored beads woven into their hair, indicating their pre-adolescent age. They were relatives of the girls currently undergoing the puberty rites mutilation. They, too, in a few years would follow their sisters into the same rites. Others, four or five in the line, were full-grown, remarkably well-proportioned young women, but with a different style of hair-do. Their shiny jet-black coiffure was divided in the middle of the skull into two thick, matted bunches standing outward above their ears, and into the hair were woven several shafts of yellow or vermilion sticks. The youngest girls wore many bark-lace rings on both legs from the ankle almost to the bend of the knee, but the older ones had only one metal bracelet around each ankle. That likewise indicated, as did their style of hair, that they had been initiated years ago. Each girl had in hand a whip several feet long, a single, strong, elastic leaf of the sansevieria plant.

As I was in the midst of framing all this in the camera view-finder, an earsplitting fracas broke out. The line of young and mature girls, like furies, dashed forward in a run toward the solid wall of silent, waiting men. Lashing whips cracked as they were wildly swung at any part of the body within reach. The males, in turn, jumped and dodged back and forth holding the sticks like fencers to protect themselves from the strokes. Screams of rage, swirling black bodies, and wildly flying, colorfully woven tresses filled the dust-churned air. There were dull thuds as blows struck the naked bodies, raising welts on arms and shoulders, and the blood dripping from narrow slits and ripped-open wounds. The men were pressing steadily forward, but never hitting back, disregarding the painful lashings and with smiles or sneers on their faces were pushing the now completely uncontrolled, hysterical line of girls toward the village entrance. My heart felt as if it were thumping in my throat. Old men and women were running back and forth, excited but not directly joining in, and amid shouted, unintelligible words, the seething lines surged closer or farther away. This went on I don't know for how long. While I held the camera close to my face and tried to keep this orgy in view, I got mixed up in the fighting, tumultuous crowd and received a whiplash across my cheek. No one cared.

Finally the lines disintegrated, but individual couples continued fighting. The courage of those young children and the wild hysteria were almost overwhelming. Yet throughout all this not a single man would either retreat or try to restrain bodily any of those infuriated females from striking him. Two of the younger girls hysterically broke down and, crying, were carried forcibly by a few of the older men who lifted them off the ground and took them, violently kicking and fighting, into the stockaded area. Then the mass of girls, steadily being pushed into the compound, gave up and just as suddenly as it started the fighting stopped.

I followed them and got into a smaller circular section where I found a whole new ceremony going on. A group of young girls were crying. Their bodies, swaying and shaking to and fro, with arms crossed over bent knees, their chins hidden between palms of their hands, formed an oval sitting group and blocked the entrance to the hut where their sisters who had undergone the operation a few days ago lay still in drugged pain. This was the "separation scene." The girls, initiated, henceforth would be accepted into the stage of mature womanhood and their younger sisters left behind as juniors were crying here as a sad realization that they could have them no longer for playmates.

This whipping ceremony is held twice during the period of initiation. The one I witnessed was the first at this camp. Later all the newly initiated girls go far away from the stockaded camp and sit a whole day under a particular selected tree which signifies fertility. From there they are forcibly carried back by the men of the tribe at the end of the day and during that time another whipping takes place. Many obscene words and epithets are hurled by the girls at the men while the lashing goes on, and it certainly seems to be a sadistic procedure. The whole thing is difficult if not impossible to explain. Maybe it is carried out on the principle of the antagonism between sexes. It could be, too, that this opportunity—to assert themselves by whipping the men—is given to these young women so that once at least in their lifetimes they will enjoy the exclusive male privilege of having the "upper hand."

These young candidates are kept in this camp for many months under intensive training and were selected before, or just at the start of, their first menstruation. They will live here under the guidance and teaching of the older "sisters" of the tribe and actually without any contact with their own mothers or elder blood sisters. They are under the tutelage of "sponsors," whose role is not only to bring them into the camp and then stay there with them, but also to lead them into the knowledge of many intricate problems of a grown-up woman. Each has a sponsor who actually reveals to her the "mysteries of life." Here she learns how to behave during menstruation and to "sit down" which means literally to sit on the ground; how to be careful never to touch food or cook for a man; in fact never to touch anything that belongs to a man during those days. She is not supposed to answer the greetings of a male during this interim. Here she will learn that she belongs to a sect which demands certain sacrifices and at the same time gives her many privileges. In addition at the same camp the teaching will go much further in other practical directions. She will learn how to extract the juice of manioc leaves and mix it with common salt and saltpeter, adding to it palm wine. This powerful and liberally mixed concoction at times is used to produce abortion. Whether the girls will, after many months of preparation, live in a communal hut or "kitchen" and have sexual liberties and a free choice about it depends entirely on the particular customs of individual tribes. But if so, it is the knowledge of the girl so educated in such camps that is supposed to protect her from becoming pregnant, since the child of an unmarried woman cannot call his father "Father." "He came from a tree," they say.

Many of the ethical and moral values in this respect are puzzling and contradictory. For instance, among some of the southern Angolan tribes a periodical examination for virginity is conducted, which is done by a few selected women in the presence of the girl's relatives, sometimes manually and sometimes using a pullet's egg. The very fact that they do demand a periodical virginity test indicates the importance which they attach to "single blessedness" accompanied by aloofness.

Again, in other areas communal living is not disapproved until tangible evidence in the form of a child complicates the affair and this, of course, then becomes a purely economic problem since a woman with child before her marriage is as undesirable as a woman without child after her marriage.

Education in the puberty camp culminates in a special act: the receipt of their final and distinguishing hair-do. Then and only then are they allowed to face the searching, gazing looks of men of the tribe. Their faces, which up to this time have been masked with a black cloth, are now uncovered and they go in a group to a nearby pool or brook where they take their cleansing bath, which physically and spiritually prepares them for the consequences of womanhood.

Here is again an example of a logical and well-founded ritual of the natives. The theories applicable to circumcision are identical to the excision on the girls. Generally children only of certain families are selected to enter these special camps. Such families belong to the sect and, as such, are bound to be loyal to each other and in every way ready to help one another. The puberty rites ceremony prepares these young girls for advancement into the succeeding stage and is naturally an unforgettable event. The operation itself is precisely parallel to the circumcision on the boys—a visible manifestation of the very fact that henceforth they will have to face the problems of adulthood with definite responsibilities. They will have to look upon the problems of sex with mature acceptance.

Thus the well-calculated, finely woven pattern of those puberty ceremonies in the girls' camps and in the boys' camps readily integrates them for their common responsibilities. A campaign for education of the initiated is undertaken to bring the young adolescent to the realization of her or his responsibilities to other members of her or his sect and toward the tribe as a unit. In both sexes a lifelong caste system is established, since members of the same age group that have been participants in the same rituals will thereafter belong to a common society—*Uganga*—meaning "Knowing Ones," and will protect each other's interests throughout life.

A society like this must be balanced logically and spiritually, where values are relative, food is meager, disease is often fatal, and life is cruel and hard. Yet how admirably those rites and rituals fit the purpose and how completely dependent is the native on them.

On the way out, as I was leaving, I saw something that made me chuckle for a long while. Men and women broke up into groups sitting around and looking over jewelry, laces, beads, and earrings brought in by a native vendor. The chief of this interesting assemblage was a heavy-set, powerfully built man. Two of his wives were adorned with all kinds of beads, shells on their backs, and single heavy brass and silverlike bracelets on arms and ankles. As he was crawling out of his hut, holding the narrow-width trap door, made from two planks and hinged a few feet above ground, he hit against the supporting Y-shaped wood with his heavy body.

Down came the door, flattening his body and dignity equally well. Both his wives loudly laughed and I had difficulty keeping a straight face to help him not to lose face. Among the others, too, some laughed, some were stone-faced, and the air was charged with expectancy.

And then unfolded a remarkable example of native sense of justice and humor. The chief slowly and calmly crawled out from under and made a sidewise pushing gesture with his left hand on his short knife, sheathed in wood, at the same time with confident eye and broad smile saying something in rapid fashion. Before I had a chance to turn to José to ask what was up, both his young and very plump wives obediently crept into the hut. He then deliberately opened the trap door attached to the supporting wood in front and on his command one of the wives started to crawl out. Just as she was on all fours, down slammed the heavy door on her. A great groan and a resounding thump indicated a flattening effect. Everybody now, including myself, rolled with laughter. Then, as she extricated herself and the second went through the same treatment, the chief was satisfied. He had evened things out.

Here in Africa evidently "what is good for the gander *must* be good for the goose."

Chapter X

DESERT GYPSIES

LATE AT NIGHT the driving was always tiring. Through the day the glaring sun and often sand driven against the windshield made it such an ordeal that by night I could hardly keep my eyes open. My hands had to clamp the steering wheel, gripping it stiffly; everything bounced up and down constantly, so my arms ached. I drove like an automaton. I was tired and had great difficulty keeping awake. South of Chibemba the narrow, winding road played hide-and-seek continually with giant boulders, coiling around them and seemingly losing itself just to pop out suddenly again. The bouncing beams of the headlights threw intermittent silver shafts into the night; hawks were flying and kangaroo rabbits jumping all around and in front of us. I knew well that I would have to drive for hours before making camp. All of a sudden I noticed a solitary figure in the middle of the road waving a rag in his hand. It was a native, his blackness merging with the surrounding inkiness.

Apprehensive, I reached for a rifle while José climbed out from the rear and came forward to investigate. In anxious tones words were exchanged and from the repeated pointing in one direction it looked as if trouble were ahead. I was told that a trekker, a Boer settler in this lonesome bush, needed help badly. In a monotonous and seemingly matter-of-fact way the native told José that his master had been lying for days very sick and helpless somewhere not far in the hills. So this faithful, simple black, after being ordered to tramp miles to reach the road, was waiting here for a chance to meet a passer-by. He had kept his lonely vigil here for the last two days like a dog devoted to his master, squatting down, huddling over a small fire, with little food and no water, just to find someone to give help. It never occurred to him to default and give up. With his simple mind and honest heart he would never think to return with a tale of futile effort.

Here I was, and I had to decide. We put the boy into the truck and started off the road and along a rough, serpentine path hewn out by the occasional use of oxcart, jounced over rocks, bushes, and sand seemingly endless. I was beaten by fatigue, and all the way wondered in what shape I would find him.

We got to a point where driving was impossible, so with flashlight in one hand, gun in the other, I started to walk. A faint beam of light ahead led me to a baobab tree with its grotesquely shaped branches etched against the sky. There a man lay. A kerosene lamp threw its feeble rays, hardly able to penetrate the heavy curtain of darkness, upon an emaciated-looking and helpless creature. He was very sick beyond doubt, as he lay on the ground wrapped in a thick, coarse horse blanket and breathed audibly. Around him were a few native women silently squatting like so many carved gnomes in this eerie light.

I talked to him. No answer. As I bent down to examine him, no one bothered even to look up. He was perspiring heavily, now and then mumbling a string of inarticulate words. I looked him over quickly and saw that he was not injured and was not bleeding. As he lay inert, sweating and in high fever, the probability of a severe malarial attack or some devastating infection came to my mind. While I was debating what to do or give to him, I smelled a pungent odor and could almost sense a sweet taste in my mouth. It came from an iron pot hanging close by over a small fire kindled with a few sticks. I went to see and it contained a concoction of grass, herbs, and twigs. This Boer had lived in the bush for years and the natives no doubt were devoted to him. He was helpless now and so they took matters into their own hands to cure him.

As I was sitting there they lifted and carried him close to the fire and the steaming pot, kept him there wrapped in the blanket while they mumbled and sang, and a few minutes later took him back again under the tree. He broke out in a profuse perspiration.

I sat and waited. He was dehydrated, in need of water and fruit, or fruit juices. It was obvious that I could not carry him with me. He was in no condition to be subjected to the bouncing of a truck for the good hundred kilometers that lay ahead. A decision had to be made. I gave him an injection of penicillin and, being uncertain about the probability that he had malaria, I left quinine with him, placed two large calabashes of water near, and tried to instruct him to drink it and wait till I sent help. A silent handshake and, if eyes could speak, an assurance that he would live were the only parting gestures.

I drove the whole night long and reached the post early in the morning, woke the *administrador*, and caused enough hullabaloo to be assured that action would follow, and then kept on going.

The high plateau region between the Cunene and Cubango rivers is north of the Kalahari Desert. Over this sandy, dry, hot, sparsely vegetated ground wander the Bushmen, "gypsies," of the African desert. The dried beds of rivers marked only by their banks crisscrossed in aimless fashion. Traveling is limited to the amount of water one can carry and distances controlled by the gasoline storage capacity. In this sandy, silent, hostile land one goes just so far and no farther. On the plains grows tough grass in which roam large numbers of elephant, rhino, and all kinds of gazelle. Kangaroo rabbits, the principal and easy meat supply of the nomadic Bushmen here, are everywhere. This interesting little animal about the size of a small Belgian hare, with very short, stunted forelegs and strong hind legs and closely resembling the kangaroo in jumping, lives in holes dug in the sandy ground and comes out after sunset.

The heat was oppressive, often close to 100° Fahrenheit, but the nights were cool. I did not see a single mosquito, but all over the white ant termites with their large and small hills were in evidence.

In the vast, desolate country in Bechuanaland, the Kalahari Desert, and here in the southern part of Angola exist seven or eight thousand of these strange little people, a slowly dying-out race. Short in stature, Mongoloid of features, with bushy hair and yellowish skin, the Bushmen live on ants, bugs, worms, eggs, wild bee's honey, roots they dig up, and meat they procure by hunting. They often trap big game such as elephant. They dig pits in places where the herds travel and feed. I had never seen any and hoped in this country to find one of them.

After much aimless wandering I selected a likely place where I was told by nearby Cunhamas that some of those little Bushmen often emerge to barter for salt. I stayed there for three days before late one afternoon they arrived. The first group I met consisted of about two dozen individuals including women and children. They came in single file into an area thickly wooded and practically impenetrable owing to the small, dense bush growth with needlelike endings on every branch.

The women wore large karosses, a leathery blanket, tied over the right shoulder and draped diagonally so that it passed under the left armpit, with a few delicate-looking beads sewn haphazardly on it. They all had children on their backs and the leader of the group, an old man, had a deep vertical cut between the eyes above the bridge of the nose—a sign of his circumcision in youth—which almost melted into the wrinkles in his parchment-like face. He came forth smiling and very shy. More gesticulation, clicking tongues, and mimicking went on. In response to my request about pitmaking a regular pantomime was performed. He dug a hole in the ground, put some sticks into the bottom of it, pointed upward, and got right into the hole himself, howling like a coyote. His performance needed no explanation.

They were friendly, banded together like a small community. Their appearance was rather degenerate and probably so because of inbreeding. The men carried bows and arrows in hand and each of the younger ones had a long, flexible bamboo pole with a sharp hook about three inches in length on the narrow, tapered end. They use this for hunting kangaroo rabbits. They stood apart like so many wary animals watching every move of mine. Many of the young women were pregnant, but their physical agility was not in the slightest diminished by their state, for their movements were lithe and easy when they rose from a sitting position or moved about.

I turned again to the band leader. Evidently he enjoyed sitting in the small hole directly on the sharp sticks, for he remained there while I tried to convey that I would like to have him or some of the others lead me, if not too far, and show me the pits they had built to trap elephants. There was violent tongue clicking, pleasant smiling, and when I showed them a sack of salt as payment for their effort, everything was quickly arranged.

The two who were selected came gesticulating, evidently planning this trap-inspection tour, but acted indifferent to my presence. At any rate the idea appealed to me. Though their poisoned arrows and spears, if many, would kill an elephant, it is a difficult and unpredictable job. They find it easier to dig a large pit many feet deep, camouflage it cleverly, and trap him in it. These they place strategically where they know the herd will feed or pass by. Deep into the ground at the bottom of such contraptions they then drive large, strong stakes four to six feet in length with sharpened spikes on the upper ends. Whatever falls into these pits dies a slow and excruciating death. They will run on their trap line almost as regularly as does an Indian in the North Country. They check up frequently to see if game has fallen in, and if they find an elephant in the pit not dead, they will finish him off in short order with their poisoned arrows and spears. They get into the pit, cut him up there, and lift him out piece by piece, divide the meat, and take the tusks, leaving only the skeleton behind.

I set out with them, having no idea how long it would take to find the pits, grabbed odds and ends, some surgical and drug stuff, cramming it into the field-glass case, and with gun in hand started to follow the two Bushmen. As usual no one seemed to be excited except me. I didn't know where I was going or when I was coming back and it mattered little by now.

The trekking was absolutely horrible. Soon there was no path and I had to follow them closely as I could. The bush was thick and among the "wait-a-bit" low branches and all kinds of thorns and creepers the going was difficult. Constantly I was hindered, stumbling, slipping, falling. They had an uncanny and expert manner of bending way down and sideways at the same time, effortlessly and seemingly tirelessly, while using short running steps. They kept on and on. One looked back occasionally as though sizing me up; the other just didn't care at all.

My hands were unprotected—I had left my gloves behind

—and soon they were sore, bleeding, and my fingernails ripped. I thought of giving up—I had had enough. Every time I reached to hold aside a branch or wild palm with serrated frond, I got hooked on thorns or nettles. My face was burning; it felt like someone had flogged me across the eye; I was hit by some plant a while back. My back ached, legs were cramped, but on I had to go. In this leather field-glass case, flopping back and forth and getting in my way, I packed syringes, morphine, penicillin, and a few scissors, needles, and catgut. Now it occurred to me how funny it was. The only time I could use those things would be if one or both my guides got hurt. That was not likely to happen. On the other hand, if *I* got hurt, what use would my tools be to those two?

I had no water with me. Stupidly I trusted that I would not need any. If I understood them rightly, the place we were heading for was not far away. I began to get thirsty. For a while I didn't mind it, but the longer I went on and the more I had to work and struggle, the more I felt the need of water. If you don't know how it feels to be without it, I hope you never need to know. Your tongue is parched, and is a chunk of obstruction in your mouth, and every time you try to swallow, it clogs the way. I tried to get saliva to swallow at least, but I found out that there was very little to collect. Soon I learned that by not opening my mouth and not breathing through it, I could preserve more moisture. But I had always had difficulty breathing through my nose owing to some deviation in my nasal septum. So when you are gasping for air in this unbearable humidity, you have little time to wonder why in the name of saints you decided to search for pits. I did not doubt that they would find the trap soon, but I wondered if they could take me back quickly—and, I hoped, alive—from there.

Something happened. Both stopped short. One jumped back a bit, and then, while pulling his short, straight-bladed knife slowly out of its wooden shield, fixed his eyes downward and quick as lightning cut into something writhing on a rotted, fallen tree trunk. It was a coiled-up python he neatly cut in half! The other just looked on. What eyes, and what self-confidence! The giant snake, cut in two, thick as my arm, still wriggled, and then a few more well-aimed strokes close to the head where the vertebrae of the neck joined and all was finished. And now both of them went into action immediately and each picked up a chunk of bloody meat like a big five-inch steak and off we went. It must be a delicacy; they didn't even bother to skin or cook it—they just bit into it and ate it raw. I forgot I was thirsty!

What next? Nothing but climbing and walking and stumbling onward; not for much longer, I hoped.

And then there was a clearing. Trees had been chopped and the sun shone through easily. Logs had been dragged through bush and brush in the sandy soft turf, leaving a natural path for game to travel.

How perfectly silly not to find the path leading to the pit now! How utterly impossible with all the trees down around here not to recognize the work of humans! How could an elephant be fooled this way?

Well, I didn't know, but I was about to see. They walked through and I followed, expecting to find the pit at any moment. I was disappointed. There was another clearing, more logs chopped and piled in a haphazard fashion to form a gatelike approach. From here on the bush looked like untouched, virgin land, no direction, no broken trees, nothing could be seen.

They stood still, listening silently. Here, on a flat, branch-covered square where the trees and low-growing bush were just naturally thick, I hardly could see, but something had surprised them. As if they grew out of the ground, like gnomes in this light-filtered glade, they listened and watched for something. The pit was ahead. I couldn't see much of it and certainly less inside. Something had fallen into it, but what? An elephant or a small gazelle? I got closer and looked down into empty darkness with unaccustomed eyes, could see no form, no clue at all.

One Bushman quickly cut some creepers and branches while the other opened up the pit more, like a well-trained team, without a word spoken, and a rope was made. I edged closer to this dark, cold emptiness and bent over. I thought, as my eyes slowly got used to it, that I could see the still blades of a few spears at the bottom among the pointed stakes. And then, "What is this thick mass close to the slanting wall of the pit?" No groan, no noise, nothing. Something was lying there, dead.

They, like monkeys, now tied the end of this crudely woven and knotted rope to one tree and climbed down one after the other into the depths. A fearfully long time elapsed before one finally emerged. Just below him the second came, carrying a crumpled, bleeding mass. They climbed over the rim and laid a terribly mangled body, a native woman, a Bushman woman, in front of me. Like dogs they laid it, like dogs retrieving a bird.

What could be done for her? She was dead, spiked through the chest and with an open, terribly gashed wound in the groin, having bled to death hours ago. The ants had already started their work. The job was finished for us and beginning for them.

No condolences to express and no words to say; no death certificate to file here. Two Bushmen standing, and the white marvels at how simple and final everything can become.

I felt sick; I wanted to go home.

I returned completely exhausted, not even anxious to know just what happened. How did this woman fall into the pit?

When I arrived, they, in businesslike fashion, had already selected a place for a primitive settlement of temporary shelters and erected it by sticking branches together to make small huts. Only women built the huts. I watched them and patiently bided my time to find out about the missing woman. The opportune moment came and José brought out another bag of salt. I gave them the salt, which they ravenously grabbed, even picking up the individual, minute grains that fell into the sand while chattering with tongues clicking as though they were giving the signal for horses to get moving. In the midst of it an almost ugly, heated argument developed among some of the old women with starved looks, snatching for possession of salt. The tongue clicking became fast and furious, but just as suddenly as the thing started, it ended, reminding one of quarreling animals, and each one, young and old, carried a handful or more of salt back to their little shelters.

Looking like a wizard, the old leader of the band then sat down, placed his feet on either side of a notched, flattened piece of wood to anchor it, and twirled a stick between his palms very fast and steadily, drilling hard into the soft wood until he made fire by friction. Another held dried grass and leaves close to it. Soon it started to smoke and burst into a little flame.

Then I turned to José and told him my story. He then asked the old man for an explanation. None came forth. Only a blank face and complete acceptance that whatever happened in the bush was natural. I wonder if this is not the same philosophy and practice that the Eskimo has. The old become useless and if, through physical weakness or mistaken judgment they lag behind, get lost, killed by a lion, or fall into a pit, it is fate, nothing but fate.

They were certainly a very primitive-looking group, with completely hairless faces and tufted hair on their heads. They had no large, fatty buttocks like the Hottentots south of here. While I was watching them, out of one of those makeshift little huts a mother brought an ostrich egg containing water and let a small toddler drink through a bamboo forming a straw. In small groups some were sitting and many were crouching on their knees munching food, perhaps delicacies like lizards, roots, grubs, and ant eggs. They did not mind me at all. I asked José to bring out some more cigarettes from the truck and we both bribed them left and right. I heard a lot about their imitation dances, that is, imitating animals or birds while they dance, and was anxious to see some of it. After much goading and purposely stimulating a few of the old ones with red wine they started. They did not dance as a group. Their drums were nothing but the gourds they use for carrying food or water. They simply turned them bottoms-up and beat on them, producing a sound rather alien to other native drums.

One man danced as a giraffe, another as a secretary bird, perhaps, and the third represented the hunter. The giraffe had some spots on him, but not black and yellow, and though his neck was short, he did his best during the dance to elongate it. The other, imitating the secretary bird, strutted up and down with both arms hanging loose at his sides, for all the world like the wings of a bird. The third, as a hunter, stalked them both with bow and arrow in hands. It was fascinating, and in watching the band sing a monotonous tune, repeating it again and again, to me it seemed like a funeral incantation for the old woman left in the bush, whose sight I could not forget.

Those Bushmen, here today and gone tomorrow, on the verge of extinction, have a multitude of fascinating, interesting habits, customs, and rites. The only memento I took away besides my notes and films was the bamboo weapon for kangaroo hunting. This I bought for half a bag of salt.

José and I headed northward into the unknown. The hunting of those kangaroo rabbits intrigued me and as I drove the truck, with José sitting in the rear, I kept thinking about those primitive Bushmen catching them with that extraordinary weapon. I made up my mind then and there that the first time I saw a rabbit we would try to catch it. Every time I cast a fishing rod I hook a branch or pick myself up with it, so casting is not my forte. But the temptation was strong. While driving along after sunset, many of those jumping hares would spring up here and there, bouncing like balls.

José had the bamboo pole, and this thing seemed to have a life of its own and a cussed desire to wiggle. Ten feet in length, it would not fit when laid in the rear of the truck. The truck, bouncing over the washboard road, started the unwieldy thing rolling, back and forth, left and right, as though possessed. We first laid it on the floor, jamming it between the bedrolls and food baskets in the back. It wiggled out. José then banged and shouted from the rear to stop. On the second attempt we let half its length stick out behind, where it drooped and flopped. It got loose again. Finally in desperation he sat on it, perhaps hugged it, maybe loved it, and surely caressed it, then fought it and pummeled it, but to no avail. I advised him to come forward into the cab with it, and now we stuck the spear of this implement boldly through the open window. Once more we started rolling, but now it whipped, looped, humped, and bent. José giggled. The native sense of humor is simple and spontaneous. Evidently he knew that this piece of long stick was too much for me to cope with. He had no responsibility with it; it was my show and his enjoyment. I had to stop again and this time tried to roll it into a coil. This was easily accomplished, but the trick was to make it stay that way.

Rabbits were jumping and skipping all around us. The challenge was here. I smiled, José smiled. We were in common accord. He knew from the moment I acquired the Bushman's weapon that sometime we would hunt with it. True, I had something more on me than a loincloth and my boots were some hindrance, and perhaps my hands and eyes were not as highly trained as those of the nomads of the southern desert, but, seeing the faithful and trusting expression of my boy, I had to proceed. *"Jacta alea esto."* "Let the die be cast."

I firmly grabbed the demonic instrument and whipped it slightly, twisting it just as if I knew why. I took a few practice swings. On the first I successfully hooked José's sun helmet. He was much impressed with this seemingly purposeful motion and the elegant ease with which I detached it from his head. I smiled and behaved as if I had executed a premeditated *coup de main* with flawless skill. With another mighty effort even more forceful than the first I nailed my second target—this time the canvas water bag. I punctured it in just the right place and lost all the water we carried in it. After such practice swings I felt experienced enough to sally forth on the hunt. My reputation was at stake and I had to catch one of those rabbits, alive or dead. I knew José expected much, though he said little.

I went into action.

Those rabbits, those rabbits, fast and unpredictable. Every time I got close and tried to snare one with the hook-like piece at the end of my weapon, it jumped sideways. I readied myself to the right and they jumped to the left. I planned on a leftward thrust and they ended up on the right. An uneven battle, but I had to continue in spite of my age, my profession, my responsibility toward my growing children. I felt obliged to stick tenaciously to the task if for nothing more than for the sake of my own pride.

But I got tired. I stopped, heaving heavily, and sat down on one small mushroom-like white anthill, scrutinizing José. Suddenly the right solution to this difficult dilemma came to me.

Regaining my normal rate of respiration, a bit relaxed, and with an air of perfect innocence, smiling reassuringly, I put a new plan into action. I winked at him in a convivial manner and put all my effort into creating the impression that I enjoyed this game, while extending the bamboo stick invitingly. I certainly did not want to usurp all such pleasures for myself, so I invited him to be a part of this noble hunt. I drew mouth-watering pictures of rabbit stew, with or without pepper, extolling it as an unforgettable delicacy, and particularly so if it were kangaroo rabbit stew. All men of all creeds and colors crave it, if José could catch one for me.

He fell for it. How inexperienced they are in the ways and wiles of civilized reasoning. He agreed and so I told him that henceforth he would have the honor of doing the catching and I would direct him. I selected a command position by climbing up on the roof of the cab. Sure enough, there not far ahead, among a small flock of guinea hens, three of those bouncing things were flirting with us. The chase was on.

They waited and waited, motionless but suspicious, as rabbits would do, ears moving back and forth. Both the hunter and the hunted were in splendid form. A stealthy stalk, closer and closer, tiptoeing, and then a sudden leap. It looked as though hook and hare would meet. But oh, no. José jumped, heaved, and dove forward, and the rabbit did the same. Everyone went in every direction. This went on many times amid my cheers.

Then the inevitable happened. In one of his lunges José stepped into a burrow, snapping our precious hunting implement in two and flattening himself like a pancake. Against fate one cannot fight. Wise and tired as we were, we agreed to let the Bushmen have the fun.

Darkness came fast and José's happily smiling countenance melted into the night as I opened up a can of South African crayfish to dine on instead of rabbit stew.

Chapter XI

NUTS AND BOLTS

CAMP WAS MADE for the night on the "kangaroo battleground." The customary nightly ritual involved climbing with flashlight into the back of the truck and, as usual, whamming my head on the kerosene lamp and plowing through odds and ends. I had a two-burner camp stove and it always lay, sooner or later, snugly underneath the end of my spine. It was not easy to extricate nets and canvas coverings, annoyingly entangled among magazines, bananas, and loose pineapples. Every night I had to check the mosquito nets and more than once spray with DDT Aerosol bombs for bugs, ticks, or mosquitoes. José became obsessed with the same idea, and if I did not watch him closely, every sunset he would get hold of the Flit gun and spray everything generously so that for hours after I sneezed and sneezed.

Morning brought the usual chore of preparing breakfast, and I like eggs, coffee, and toast for mine and dislike giving up these, even when in Angola. I had powdered eggs and if I watched the amount of water to be mixed with them, they could pass for home-style scrambled eggs. With Borden's coffee powder and Pream one could have excellent coffee, and the saccharine tablets sweetened both my disposition and the coffee as well. True, occasionally my scrambled eggs looked like molasses and tasted like unleavened bread dough, and true, at times my rolls were dehydrated and were the consistency of cement, yet good coffee could wash down many things in Angola.

We finished eating and washed the dishes with little water and much sand, after which everything was packed back again. This was a trying chore, accompanied by much fervent cussing. Order and system could not be kept and finally the entire mess looked like a giant, full wastebasket. But it was finished and so I climbed into the front, José into the back; I sat erect, he lay down; I had shoes on my feet, he had none; I kept mine on the foot pedals, his dangled limply, sticking out of the canvas-covered rear, and we drove on.

Who was the more fortunate?

After many weeks of wandering together, enduring hardships, staying in the bush for days without water to drink, trying to keep up with evasive Bushmen, hunting for meat, trying to get out of swampland or quicksand, and listening to my profanity in English, José knew that I needed rest, reassurance, and tender care. When we arrived at Sá da Bandeira and I got a room in the only hotel available, he came and explained in a smattering of English, mixed with Portuguese and some Umbundu, that he must buy some cloth for his first, second, third, or fourth wife, I am uncertain which, and that it would cost one hundred twenty angolares, or about four dollars. Since we never talked about monetary matters and both of us felt that among men like ourselves money didn't mean anything, certainly not enough to put any distrust between us, he and I had no previous arrangement regarding the amount I would pay him for his services, and whether weekly, monthly, or by the year.

This was the first time he had asked for money. Without hesitation I gave it to him. I knew only too well he had no intention of buying calico for his wives. His throat was parched, his spirits were low, his eyes were wandering, and his hands were slightly shaking. So what is better medicine for that than some kaffir beer? I gave him the hundred twenty angolares and let him go.

I bumped into a geologist and we decided to spend a few pleasant hours in the only movie in this part of southern Angola. I offered to take him and his wife, but to my surprise we couldn't get into my truck. José in his customary protection of my paraphernalia in the cab of the truck had locked both doors and taken the key with him. Fortunately I had a second key, so we drove to the movie.

It was midnight when we returned to the hotel and in the long, rather dark corridor we three bid good night to each other. As I turned toward the direction of my quarters, I caught a glimpse of two faces peering through the slit of a swinging door. Even in the shadows I recognized the smiling countenance of José and another native boy behind him. At that moment I felt that I must show my authority as a white man and José's boss. I took out my duplicate keys, shook them firmly under his nose while verbally chastising him for removing the key from the cab and taking it with him on his jaunt.

At that he smiled in agreement and said, "*Sim, senhor.*"

"Now never do this again," said I sternly. "I trusted you and I took good care of you. I even gave you money to buy some calico for your wives and look what you did! You went off and took the key with you and I couldn't have gone to the movies unless I had this second key!" and I shook it again under his nose.

He said, "*Sim, senhor.*"

"Enough of this," I snapped. "Go get a good sleep and I will see you tomorrow."

Then I turned toward my door, opened it, and walked in. As I put on the light, I stared in astonishment. There was one of the duskiest and loveliest maidens waiting for me, sitting stiff as a board on a chair. My poor José, my only friend in Angola, my trusted boy! Now I understood him. Evidently he had spent all evening hunting a maiden for me and with the help of the houseboy, using a duplicate key, they placed this bait in my room. How many hours she had waited there and which of us was the more embarrassed I don't know. I broke out in a laugh, fished out a couple of paper angolares from my pocket, and pushed them into her hands, whereupon she said, "*Sim, senhor.*" But she didn't make a move to leave. She stood waiting, probably assuming I was paying her in advance. Moments passed. Finally I opened the door, patted her on the shoulder, which I am afraid she also misunderstood, and got her out of my room, to my great relief.

Next morning José and I climbed into the truck. He looked at me with a quizzical and much-confused expression. In fact all day he watched me carefully from the corners of his eyes. Every once in a while he acted as though he thought I was sick. He offered me wine with great solicitude, he didn't let me exert myself, and he was visibly puzzled.

Like the matter of money, we never talked any more about this. There are certain things in life that men do not talk much about and this was one of them.

That José! He was really a wonderful boy.

We were on the way from Sá da Bandeira northward in search of more rituals. Actually I was looking for a circumcision camp I heard was established somewhere in the bush halfway between Sá da Bandeira and Quipungo. We traveled rather aimlessly. By now I accepted with resignation the state of the roads and knew that I could hardly expect to make more than a few hundred kilometers a day. My boy, always cheerful and constantly humming some tribal song —always the same one—helped to take the "ups and downs" with gaiety. To maintain balance under such difficulties required a great amount of concentration and, I might say, correct timing while driving. José seemed to be better equipped for such a bumpy journey. Atop his head his highly cherished white tropical sun helmet, reinforced with his underwear packed inside as a space-saving measure, absorbed the jolts and shocks. He enjoyed this roller coasting and each time a dull thud indicated that my timing was not exactly right he glanced over his shoulder with a broad smile, trying to reassure me that all this could be worse.

So merrily we rolled along and I was just getting into the rhythm of things when a "light" sensation came over my driving. That I had the steering wheel fast in my hands there was no doubt, but neither could there be any doubt that this same wheel was detached from something it should be fastened to. Then, too, I noticed nuts and bolts and other similar trifling appurtenances loosened from the dash-board.

Here again, José was in a more enviable position than I. This child of Africa knew not enough to be worried, but just enough to trust. "What of such trivial matters as a loosened, rattling wheel, and after all, it is in the 'white man's' hand. Haven't they proved time and time again that they can master any situation for us? Didn't my *senhor* come along with this exciting-looking, red-colored monster from a country far across the big water? It certainly must be well built and safe. He knows what to do at the right time and the right place, and so why worry, why care? I, José, his boy, shall only relax and enjoy the ride. Sure, he does look a bit funny hanging onto the loose wheel and pulling it up, down, and sideways without changing our direction toward that ditch, but why be concerned?"

Then we stopped, rather abruptly, I should say, but at least right side up in a ditch. This was the only time my José lost his dignity, and with it his sun helmet. Comb, soap, handkerchiefs, and socks spilled out and all over him. I, too, felt slightly squeezed under an avalanche of bags, boxes, guns, and ammunition, all this mingled with English tea biscuits, cans, and with a large variety of assorted jams and marmalades. We were stationary.

I was not pinned to the steering wheel; on the contrary the wheel was pinned down by me. I climbed out, holding the darned thing in my hand for safekeeping. England's best tea biscuits, Borden's powdered coffee, DDT powder, and kerosene oil, mixed with Carnation milk, with films and ammunition, were scattered everywhere. The truck was not damaged, neither was our spirit daunted. It was about noon and since little could be done under such circumstances we both agreed to take advantage of the fact that the food got unpacked.

The menu offered a great variety, with liberal chance for selection. After eating I studied my truck's and our position and ruefully admitted to myself that in relation to the road and direction I was to travel, we were now slightly deviated. I slid under the chassis to see how we could lift the truck out, gave that up for the time being, and, crawling out from under, noticed that from the bush had emerged something resembling a couple of Crusaders. Both wore a short skin skirt just reaching to the knees and were bedecked with various shell decorations painted in different colors, with beads and brass bracelets on their legs and arms. These two jet-black, tall, and thin Methuselahs, carrying spears in their hands and bows and arrows across their shoulders, came with nonchalance. One looked almost Caucasian, with a goatee-like beard and hair flowing freely to his shoulders. The other had a close-cropped beard all over his chin, showing some gray here and there, and likewise with long black hair, glossy from butter or fat smeared on it. Certainly both were picturesque and their agility belied their ages. They approached us with a certain hesitation and shyness, stopped a few yards away, took stock of us and the situation, and lost no time in concluding that something worth investigating had happened here. I, trying to make the best of a bad situation, since they were photogenic enough, decided to film them.

When I returned from the truck with a handful of cigarettes kept specifically for making friends, José already had them engaged in a lively conversation. We learned that they were on a lion hunt. The village to which they belonged had recently lost women and children to marauding lions. They decided either by their own choice or by the selection of the tribe to track down the lions. They seemed extremely self-confident, but, looking them over and sizing up their rather useless regalia, I was not so sure I agreed with them. At any rate now they had decided to pause and rest. Where could be found a more appropriate spot for it than near such interesting humans as José and I were in their eyes? We were under intensive and critical scrutiny. From their extensive gesticulation I knew something was in the air. As they sat with bent knees and crossed legs, facing each other and engaged in animated conversation, they looked like two windmills revolving at a mad pace in opposite directions. I asked José what was up and he announced that they wanted to entertain us with a dance. The rascals had something on their minds. Although the native will dance for all occasions, sorrow, happiness, birth, and so on, in this case, the offer was unsolicited.

Upon questioning their story was that the good spirits showed them that they were on the right track, since it was a positive and auspicious sign to have happened upon us while on their hunt. I, for my part, was unable to understand their reasoning unless we were looked upon as easy prey for marauding lions—and that could well be the case.

Only too willing to agree to the dance, I hurried to get camera and films ready. I had hardly set my equipment in order when another hubbub arose with more pointing of spears, arrows, and swords—all in my direction.

"What now?" I asked José.

My boy sheepishly divulged the meaning of their motions. Those sly rogues were saying that they knew the lions were somewhere nearby and that the hunt would be successful, but they also advised us that the good spirits protecting them, and particularly us, under these circumstances would be more favorably disposed toward us if a few more cigarettes could be doled out. Also there must be something in our strange basket-woven carafe, perhaps a different kind of spirit for them to taste. It is remarkable how intuitive a child of nature can be. For the sake of boosting my morale as well as theirs we gave them a few drinks.

A bunch of North American Indians on the warpath could never match the whooping and cavorting of that light-footed pair. Dancing into the air, leaping over bushes, or jumping right into them, they brandished their swords and sent spears and arrows flying. Engrossed in filming, I was unaware that more than once my head, at least my hair, was dangerously close to being shaved. Then, as a finishing touch to this remarkable exhibition, with perfect aim they threw their spears into a sturdy, rugged tree trunk. An indescribable look of dismay crossed their faces when, upon pulling out their spears, they found the razor-sharp edges completely spoiled.

Then came a rest. We induced them, with more cigarettes and wine, to give us a hand in lifting the truck out of the ditch. We chopped down trees for logs, we pried, lifted and rested, heaved and rested, pulled and rested, pushed and finally managed to get it out of the ditch. Then without a single word they disappeared, silently walking along a narrow path leading into the mysterious bush of Africa and leaving behind the picture of two brave lion hunters.

I found bolts and nuts with screws and pins lying in disorder on the floor board. In viewing the matter objectively a dejected steering wheel and drooping wires, possibly important, connected with heater or speedometer, are a sorry sight indeed. The entire matter looked hopeless—wheel, nuts, bolts, José and myself included. I had to do something. According to maps, we were about fifty kilometers from the nearest trading post and though we could camp out and stay where we were, sooner or later we would have to go. The sooner it was, the better, and so I acted boldly and tried to show up as well as I could to José. I took out a couple of monkey wrenches carried for just such occasions, the sight of which stirred considerable interest in him. Therefore, I felt morally obliged to explain to him what I intended to do with them. His inability to understand much English helped me greatly.

I set to work, in no time at all connected several things with several other things. I inserted some bolts so I could put some nuts on them. With a determined motion and perseverance I attached the steering wheel to some formidable-looking shaft coming through the floor board. I took it for granted that this unorthodox mechanical repair would suffice and counted the operation a success.

Proud of my accomplishment, including a pinched finger and a lost nail, I packed the monkey wrenches away. We proceeded to reload the jeep with kerosene, DDT, ammunition, films, baking powder, canned beans, dehydrated potatoes, evaporated milk, and a multiplicity of tea biscuits. Why do the English always pack them in those confounded tin boxes so that, once opened, you can never cram back the same amount again? I do not know!

Chapter XII

THE BUSHMEN

OTHER ROVING BANDS of Bushmen were somewhere on the banks of the Cuchi River. Those are the most northern bands, having penetrated slowly upward and away from the desert perhaps through centuries.

Senhor Bretaan, a well-known white hunter and trader, and Dr. Gilchrist from the mission joined me. We had with us his tape recorder and a single-cylinder, air-cooled, gasoline-driven power unit in order to record the very unusual and distinctly characteristic tongue-clicking language of the bands. This unique manifestation of speech intrigued me greatly.

Relations between José and myself ever since the "kangaroo" hunt were a bit strained. Whenever I had to stop to take a drink or check tires and radiator, he would climb down from his quarters and somewhat perfunctorily help me do what was needed. Immediately afterward, however, he deliberately would go back again to the rear, bluntly ignoring me.

For the purpose of covering more mileage in a day we did not stop for a midday meal. My chief concern was to prevent diarrheas, both bacillary and amoebic, particularly common in Angola, and so we tried to avoid native food and often lived on oranges and bananas only. The light green leaves of banana trees always indicated a native settlement and there one could get those delicious small plantains. They were tree-ripened, very tasty, and safe to eat since one peels the skin, unwrapping the clean fruit. For like reasons oranges were desirable, juicy, and refreshing. We could conveniently carry pineapples for days and longer, letting them roll freely back and forth on the floor board and ripening themselves in such a painful way.

The native almost everywhere here exists on corn, ground and pounded into mash, on manioc, and dried beans. Children eat fruits, if available. It was a common sight to see women and children congregating on the hillsides around a large, flat slab of granite where they grind and pulverize the tough kaffir corn into flour and then carry it on their heads in calabashes miles away to their villages. There, they mix it with some water or milk, and the resulting mush is their universal food. They eat it morning, noon, and night, and they often cook it with the juice of boiled beans. They simply ladle it out with the curved palm of the hand.

A glance at their faces, hands, and protruding bellies, spindly legs, pale, soft, and scanty hair, apparent apathy, makes one ask, "What ails them?" Many things, including infestation with worms, malaria, sleeping sickness, yaws, and so on. One thing stands out clearly: many of them, literally thousands, have a protein deficiency that then, as a definite clinical entity, presents its picture, a condition, an illness, crippling and debilitating, very severe nutritional disorder, *kwashiorkor*—a deficiency, protein deficiency. Consequently no amount of vitamins given to them will cure it. Children, mostly infants, get sick from it, very sick, and have a high mortality rate. This strange name of this almost universally known disease is borrowed from an African tribe. Only recently, through a twist of fate, was an answer found how to cure it, or to prevent it. All primitives in Africa and, too, in the southern part of Asia and even in Central America, living on maize, corn, bananas, yams, and cane sugar—all very low in protein content—might develop it.

Because the British, through a mistake, sent a large shipment of skim milk to Uganda instead of powdered whole milk, the entire lot of children and infants receiving it miraculously got better, and so it was found that the high fat content of the powdered whole milk kept increasing symptoms of diarrhea and debility, whereas the fat-poor skim milk turned out to be the cure. Fish, meat, milk, beans, and groundnuts will prevent it. But how often can the natives here get those?

When groping and trekking through the bush you stumble upon a tribe so noticeably sick, weakened, and lethargic that even their leaders, the men of mature age responsible for hunting, fishing, getting food for the rest of them, just sit down, staring at nothing and belching under the mercilessly beating sun, then they probably have the deficiency. Little acreage, a few cleared patches here and there showing corn, maize, and tapioca plants, barely any fruit trees, no cattle on the fields, no chickens scratching under foot.

What is the answer?

If they live close to rivers their diet may include fish,

which generally is dried on the roofs of their huts. There is little hunting done by the Ovimbundus, more among the Cheokwees, and very much more among the Bushmen. Game meat is scarce, and with the exception of fish they have little chance of getting animal protein. Indeed many of the tribes show severe protein deficiencies.

We traveled in this sparsely inhabited country, and instead of measuring the distances by miles we counted the number of hours and days to reach a resthouse or a lonesome mission. Schedules and routines were certainly thrown overboard. One starts early always; it is cool then and more mileage is covered before the sun gets hot. After eleven o'clock the heat is oppressive. Then is the time to stop under a large tree. The butane gas stove starts quickly and if it is set up so that a breeze does not interfere, in a few minutes water boils. It is an advantage over an open fire. A cup of hot tea or coffee is ready in an instant.

Meat I always carried, salted or boiled game, duiker- or steinbok I had shot and cut into strips, then dried in the sun. José did the cooking and I the seasoning. He continually mixed the egg powder with the dehydrated potatoes and served it as scrambled potatoes. I also had a considerable number of canned fruits and vegetables. However, to my great distress I had some struggles with them. My good friends in the States had given me a can opener, believing, gullible soul that I am, that this small, compact-looking article with a couple of wheel-like projections and a gripping arrangement is a traveler's most indispensable tool. I was never instructed how to use it. I don't remember if there were written directions with it, but I do remember that I never could open a single can with it. I put it against the top, I applied it to the bottom. I rotated it clockwise and counter-clockwise. I never even scratched the can. It was like a crossword puzzle: it made me cross and it made me puzzled. Only my trusted Swedish jackknife could open a can and I had success with peaches and pears, but when I attacked a small can of sardines, by the time I got through they were sufficiently chopped up to pass for anchovies.

One of the boys who assisted carrying some of the film packs, cameras, and such was always a wandering soul. I never knew his name, but for my own satisfaction called him "Friday." He was forever in places he had no cause to be, under my feet when he should be close to my hands, and "on my hands" when he should be somewhere else . . . perhaps far away, and I mean far away. I don't think he ever took a bath in his life.

I was camping close to the river and as one morning I climbed out of the truck, getting things in order to film, my "Friday" rushed in with arms and hands going like a Dutch windmill and with all his thirty-two white teeth showing. I didn't understand him, and José was not around, so I shoved a camera into his hands, hoping that it would shut him up. No, not this one. He got more excited, shook the camera up and down, held it up to his eyes and rolled them wildly in one direction, pointing with foot and hand. Something was happening and so I went to see.

The boy, gingerly stepping back and forth, kept hitting the grass and bushes with a long stick. I knew that there must be a snake. The native is clever enough to know that most snakes are timid and many sluggish. If one makes enough noise in the bush and disturbance in the grass, they will start to get away.

I followed him and thought of all sorts of hair-raising consequences. We had not gone too far when he stopped as if frozen, just staring ahead. A large ringhals cobra, with white rings encircling the black neck, was coiled on top of a small anthill, swaying his head slowly to and fro. Those cobras, as scared as I am of them, are fascinating in their ugliness. The head looks exactly like a bird's. The snout and mouth end in a pointed section and the eyes are back. When alarmed they raise up from the ground a foot or two, neck widened by the hood so that it looks like a large, oval-shaped shell underneath the white rings. They are certainly something to behold.

So *that* was what my boy was saying all the time. The camera was at hand, and I tried to film. I measured the distance quickly and, praying that it was a safe distance, read the light meter and slowly raised the camera to get the snake in the view finder. Then something happened I had read about, heard about, knew about, but never hoped to see. Like a whip, the cobra raised its head suddenly backward and simultaneously jetted a whitish fluid plunk into the boy's eyes.

For seconds I was so surprised I just stood there dumfounded. In a few minutes one eye was completely closed and soon both of them badly swollen. He could not see, he could not walk, and while he howled and cried, I had to help him back to camp. I had never seen anything like this.

At camp I laid him down, tried to open the eyelids; the

eyes were terribly bloodshot; a milky fluid covered both pupils, and he was obviously in great pain. The other boys around camp talked about using milk against the "spitting cobra." I didn't have any, so first I washed the eyes out with water and then the best I could do was to make a solution of powdered milk with water and use that. How much help it was I don't know.

He lay down on the ground and refused to be moved, refused to eat, and was lethargic. We nursed him for two days. I am sure that the venom by simply getting into the eyes could not act as a poison in the entire body, but the inflamed eyes and the pain in them was too much. Ophthalmic pontocaine, an anesthetizing agent, helped ease it, and then slowly the eyes did get better. That it did hurt him very, very much I am sure, since ordinarily a native does not show signs of emotion over such matters and particularly dislikes to exhibit suffering from pain in front of a white man.

I went back and measured the distance, and from the anthill where the snake was to where the boy stood was eleven feet.

I am not the only one possessed with the fear of snakes and not the only one who becomes neurotic about them. My good friend, John Jonas, second eldest of the five famous Jonas brothers in the U.S.A., all outstanding artists and sculptors of animals, told me a story. He was in Africa one year. He, too, had heard much about the snakes, listening to horrid stories and fearful consequences, sudden death, and particularly the unpredictable behavior of the mamba, green when young, living on trees and camouflaged with the leaves, black when old, nesting on the ground. Aggressive and deadly poisonous, with a sleek black, narrow head, it strikes with the speed of lightning. It's the only snake that will never retreat.

Well, one night my good friend John went to bed. In his tent he carefully sat down on his cot, took off his boots and put them where snakes could not get into them, pulled off his trousers, sprayed underneath his mosquito netting to get rid of bugs—he was a methodical soul—blew out his candle, and climbed into his sleeping bag, snakes very much on his mind.

And then he felt the cold and slimy touch of something.

"There I am, Andy, my boy, frozen solid, scared to death, not daring to move. My left foot touches him. I can feel his slimy body. I know he is coiled up and must have gotten in sometime during the evening to get warm. Snakes are apt to do that. Now my time has come. What can I do? I don't dare move. The beads of perspiration come out all over me; I'm paralyzed with fear and can't think. Somehow I instinctively feel that if I don't move, he will not bite. How long can I stand it? I don't dare to scream; I don't dare to call for help, and what help would I get? I hear my boys happily chattering while sitting close to their fire, and here I am, about to die. I pray and swear alternately, wait motionless, how long I don't know. But I do know, Andy, that I wish I had never come to Africa. Then slowly I regain my ability to think and try to reason.

"This snake must be pretty sluggish—after all, I am still not bitten. He is coiling up comfortably and warm under the cover of my sleeping bag. So if I could only move out slowly and get my foot away, I will then jump, reach a gun, blast my bag, the snake, and with it this whole African trip of mine away. Still I didn't dare to move. That cold, icy promise for eternity touching my foot just paralyzed me. But after all—after all, I cannot stay with this snake all night. One of us has to move, and I had better be the first.

"Slowly, so imperceptibly that I, myself, could not tell if I was moving, I got my leg away. Bit by bit the contact lessened, and then I jumped . . . desperately I jumped. Once outside the bag and off my cot, I grabbed a shotgun and where I thought the snake must be I shot right straight through everything with both barrels. I reloaded and ripped open the bag.

"Andy, what do you think I saw? There was my poor flashlight—shot to bits!"

Cuchi is a small settlement of a few white Portuguese including Senhor Bretaan's home, and the headquarters of the chefe. A few typical dwellings sprawled around. The white-washed walls, blinding under the brilliant sunlight, were constructed of thick stone and cement and covered with corrugated red tin roofs that attracted the heat and absorbed it like an oven. In delicate pink or red tint, with solid, heavy wooden shutters closed protectively across the windows, the houses were clustered around a few eucalyptus trees.

There is always a man standing motionless in a doorway, face half covered under a white sun helmet, and there is always a fat white woman standing beyond him, peering out inquisitively, eager to be a part of any conversation developing between whites in this lonesome and desolate bush life. There are always five, six, seven, or eight children, dark-skinned, often with surprisingly beautiful features, peeking out, too, somewhere from beyond. And there is *always* a good-looking, young native girl in the background who either cooks or feeds pigs, chickens, or the chained monkey within this high-walled, dirty square of a back yard. She belongs to this scene just as much as the man or his wife or the children and the chained monkey. She is the all-purpose help, as the mulatto child playing near her testifies.

Every house has its square patio rear yard entirely enclosed by a high brick, cement, or clay wall, painted white or brilliant blue. The privy is placed with flagrant disregard for the principles of sanitation, close to where the cooking is done. Goats, dogs, pigs, and chickens have free run of the yard. Cages with chirping birds are hanging all around. Seldom does the trader own a cow and only the more prosperous possesses a primitive icebox, which is a galvanized-tin container with a capacity of two or three cubic feet and with access from the top. Wire mesh holds the charcoal all around it and it is thoroughly watered twice a day. The evaporation keeps the tin box cool.

We climbed out of the truck, stiff-legged, and went through the international format of greetings and smiles, entered a shaded, dark, and cool room. This was used as a store. On the dirty clay floor crude axes and hoes leaned against stacked-up yards of calico and cheap printed Indian cotton, and there were piles of tobacco and some cigarettes beside empty, rattling kerosene lamps. Here and there a few old, antiquated cans of American products, some fresh fruit, fish, and a few sacks of corn and beans could be seen. We had to push our way through some of those ever-present natives who just seem to be there from morning to night.

Bretaan knew where the Bushmen were and was reasonably sure that he could locate them. He told me that this particular group makes contact off and on with the Cheokwees similarly to the way the band I met in the south makes contact with the Cunhamas. I was willing to wait any number of days until he could pack up, organize, and go into the bush with me, which meant leaving his small trading post for about a week.

The following afternoon everybody was ready to leave. Bretaan and his wife, Dona Nazarene, a few of his personal boys, Cheokwees, and a large dog, vicious and useful for the country into which we were heading, completely filled his car. Gilchrist and I, with José and a few more Cheokwees, who nonchalantly attached themselves to the rear of my truck as ballast, followed them.

Late the next morning the headwaters of the river were reached, where we set up a permanent camp and soon established direct contact with a small Cheokwee village. Bretaan and I went out to hunt and shot a roan and a reedbuck. The camp was well established when we arrived back. Places were cleared off, trees chopped down, the high grass cut with *panga,* a vicious-looking, broad bladed, two-foot-long knife, and fire was cheerfully burning in front of our tents. José, with beaming face, was in the midst of scrambling egg powder and Dona Nazarene was baking a cake. It was a chocolate cake! I had not eaten cake for the past months.

To smell it was enough to throw one into ecstasies. Africa can be so beautiful!

That same night a great feast and dance were held among the Cheokwees and a message was relayed to the Bushmen about our presence there. They knew Bretaan, who frequently shot elephants and gave them the meat.

Sure enough, next morning and just at sunrise, a small band of strange-looking, primitive, small-statured yellowish people in single file emerged from grass as high as their eyes. They stood for a while not too far from our camp like a cluster of frightened animals, but with frequent, kind smiles on their shining faces. Then Bretaan and Dona Nazarene walked up to them talking Cheokwee and they replied with a lively clicking and clucking of tongues while their faces, as in bas-relief, rippled with a hundred wrinkles in the sunlight, accentuating the deep furrows under their eyes and around their mouths.

A strong-looking old man watched this with dignity, holding a large gourd pipe on which he drew deeply every so often and released a cloud of steel-blue smoke like a volcano, coughing spasmodically. He was the leader of the band. Soon they all sat down and just looked. Then a violent smoking contest started. Everybody smoked, since everyone had cigarettes given to him. Even very young ones knew how to enjoy the pleasure of inhaling and exhaling.

Dona Nazarene patiently viewed the scene and finally a Cheokwee translator with whom she could converse fluently found one young Bushman who understood enough Cheokwee to form a connecting link. Here was a chance to get some of this unusual tongue-clicking language to record. The microphone was placed the full 150-foot-line length away from the humming motor and the experiment began.

I spoke English; Gilchrist spoke English and Portuguese; Dona Nazarene spoke Portuguese and Cheokwee; her native spoke Cheokwee and Bushman; and the Bushmen spoke God knows what. Taking it word by word and repeating it again and again with a great deal of patience and effort, we were able to register basic words such as *earth, sky, trees, water, lions, elephants, snakes, crocodiles, men, women, stars,* and *moon.* The majority of those words begin or end with a clicking sound as the tip of the tongue hits the hard palate. The velocity of their click-clucking increases with their degree of excitement, and if tongues can be fractured, that should do it.

Here were primitives, exposed to one recent product of our modern age. If they were surprised, confused, or talked about it, they did it with reservation and certainly without showing it to us. When we played back to them the recorded words, to which they listened intelligently, they looked happy and smiled, but displayed little amazement. Their matter-of-fact attitude was baffling. What makes these people accept such seemingly impossible procedures as bringing back their own voice and words, and not show any surprise? What is going on in their minds? How do they absorb it and how do they account for all this? Was it because they believe that the white man is able to do anything and everything? Or was it because they live in a different world of their own and such alien matters as sound recorders, gasoline motors mean nothing to them? Who can say?

Under the glittering dome of African constellations I went to sleep, only to wake up the next morning and find not a single little gnome anywhere. They had disappeared as silently as they came; the only reminder of their erstwhile presence was the circle of empty little desolate huts and tiny gray ash mounds.

Chapter XIII

GIANT SABLE

In AN AREA as large as Connecticut, wedged between the Cuanza and Luando rivers, lives the noblest of all African antelopes, the giant sable. For grace and beauty none surpasses it. Its cousin, the common sable, roams all over the Rhodesias and in Tanganyika; though a truly fine animal, too, it can hardly be compared for length of horns, size of body, color of skin, and temperament with the giant sable. Not many have had the luck to see and film them. They are very few in number, probably no more than three or four hundred at most, and becoming more scarce with every passing year. They are now "royal game," and so at least are given a chance to survive. The head of the Veterinary and Game Department, Dr. Abel Pratas, an outstanding conservationist, has exercised his influence in the formulation and passage of proper laws for their protection.

In Luanda I was warned about the difficulties I would encounter. The rainy season had just ended, all rivers were high, pontoon bridges were washed away, making it near to impossible to cross the swift, half-mile wide Cuanza. *Picadas,* a suggestion of a path leading from somewhere to nowhere, were beyond reach and impassable. I was forced to wait till August and try to approach the area from the south instead of from Malange in the north. All authorities were notified and requested to facilitate my effort. Without my knowledge, for six weeks, no doubt under trying conditions, natives under the supervision of the sepaios had been working to cut a road and sufficiently clear the bush in an exceptionally wild and little-explored area so that I could reach it.

In the middle of August I started from the Dondi Mission with Dr. Gilchrist. He not only knew the country, but spoke the native language, Umbundu. Without him I might just as well have skipped the undertaking entirely.

Spring, the rainy season, was coming, yet, though bone-dry, without a drop of rain ever since May, the ground was literally covered everywhere with beautiful, short-stemmed, delicate pink and blue flowers, and the trees with brilliant red and green leaves. The source of moisture for all this vegetation is difficult to figure out—it is perhaps from heavy dew. Everything was bursting with sudden growth and splashes of color.

We came to the Chilesso Mission one evening. Duane Waln and his wife offered hospitality. It certainly was pleasant and relaxing. Dusty and dirty, I hardly could wait to bathe in the natural hot springs of the mission. We wandered among giant frogs leaping all around and croaking in an orchestra under tropical trees. Then we found the little whitewashed single-room house built directly above the springs. The water flows under the walls in and out, forming a large, natural bath tub. It was hard not to go to sleep in it, it was wonderful.

Next morning, Sunday, I saw Dr. Cushman, a remarkable old lady who has spent her entire life building up this mission hospital. In her wards I saw the sick on the beds and the relatives underneath, sleeping there through the night and doing the cooking and laundry during the day outside in front of those primitive huts where everyone works to help the other. She taught the natives, trained the native nurses, and brought a dozen or more simple boys through years of patient effort to the point of efficiency and ability, not only to assist with her operations, but to perform them by themselves under her supervision. Under primitive and difficult conditions here in the bush native nurses, girls, and young boys work efficiently in her hospital. They attend to the sick, sterilize instruments in the operating room, measure and administer medicine, make notes of illness, and often help to diagnose it. Without any anatomical knowledge and with little or no training in pathology, merely through the years of apprenticeship they have learned to operate on hernias and take care of lacerations, amputations, and appendectomies with skill. This fine old doctor, with eighty years upon her stiffened body, is bent and tired, but not in spirit. She is unable to move her head upward and is limited in her motion and ability to use her arms. So now she just stands by, watching.

I went to the mission church for the service. Native people, children, girls, and boys from the mission school, and the elders of the village were all there. The simple, whitewashed walls of the church in a light, sunny, airy atmosphere took them in like a mother embraces her countless children. The podium, severely plain and constructed from raw planks by crude carpentry, the old hand-grind organ in the corner, and the cross on the wall stood apart from the rows of benches. Silently the youngest little girls, with shiny clean faces and bright, beady eyes, leading the taller, older ones, marched in through the aisles without noise, giggling, or laughter in their washed, pert, yet simple and cheap dresses. Next the boys came and took the other rows, then the grownups came in line with solemn faces, and lastly ourselves and Dr. Cushman. She sat in front of the organ and fumbled with the music sheets, unable to read the notes if placed normally on the rack because of the stiffness in her body; she therefore kept the music in her lap. Her attention was divided between the notes and the young barefoot native boy grinding that wheezing organ. Swallows were flying back and forth, swooping low, and darting through the open slits in both walls close to the rafters, cheerfully dropping their greetings all over the worshiping crowd.

A serious-looking native predikant began the service in Umbundu and the lady doctor started to play the organ. The music filled the air. There was a strange silence, a hesitation, and no singing. The honest face of the old native preacher showed embarrassment. Evidently something was going wrong, but not with the doctor and not with her music. Melodies were flowing, at times in an uneven tempo since the boy was working hard on the organ handle. The swallows were chirping above.

Then haltingly, tactfully, with shy hesitation the minister bent down from the podium close to Dr. Cushman, with shaking fingers pointing out something in his hymnbook. The good doctor ignored all this, continued playing, now glancing onto her lap at the notes, now looking up to instruct the boy, and her strikingly sculptured, impressive white bony hands were gliding slowly and with difficulty over the keyboard. Minutes passed in silence and hesitation—the congregation seemed to be lost and did not join in.

She stopped. A few more words spoken in whispers, and then, with all the combustible temper of a young prima donna, the good lady closed the sheaf of music abruptly, reached for her own prayer book and hymnal, got up with difficulty, taking her time, and slowly moved to a chair joining us, sat down, and started to sing.

Everyone joined in with relief. The situation was saved. She played the wrong hymn, but refused to be directed or corrected. Either that or none for this Sunday!

The service went on and when music was again needed and a hymn to be sung, the old lady went back to the little dusty organ and her failing eyes scanned the starting chords of the music on her lap while the barefoot native boy ground on the handle again. Music was everywhere, rafters and walls echoed, swallows and sparrows joined in the prayer.

At noon we set out and late in the evening reached Chitau. There Bodley, a Plymouth Brethren, and his wife took us in. He is not only the "gatekeeper" for the good and bad wandering bodies and erring souls, natives and whites alike, but undoubtedly the best-informed hunter and student of wildlife in this wide and little-known part of Africa.

The road ahead was long and arduous; we had to leave Chitau early, reached the Cuanza at ten o'clock, and crossed it on a rickety pontoon ferry. The river is very wide and swift here, with formidable rapids. The ferry was nothing but four primitive dugouts lashed together side by side. The placid, lackadaisical native crew, three of them, were pulling for all they were worth on a spliced cable loosely tied to trees on both banks. The unsalty navigators and the flimsy craft shot the rapids.

Once across, much happier, we kept on driving farther north and reached the post of the *chefe*. He and his young wife were newcomers to the lonesome bush. They offered us with open arms the best they could muster up. We stayed here in hope that the *administrador* would soon come and meet us. He could be much help. We waited and waited (not unusual in Angola) and tried to locate our lost man in the outside world. Every morning with an American walkie-talkie we cranked and cranked, getting crankier and crankier with each failure to make contact.

At the end of the third day, not only my patience, but our time was running short, and so in the morning we climbed into the truck again. José and a sepaio who was supposed to guide us, helping to find a camping place, got into the rear of the truck and off we went.

This time I left my rifles behind and the only weapon with us was Gilchrist's 9-mm. Luger pistol. Knowing that the sable is "royal game," shooting of which is forbidden, I wanted to show the officials my good intentions. Being uncomfortably close to man-eating lions more than once in the next few days, I later felt sorry about this foolhardy decision.

About eighty kilometers away we reached a crossroad. There we turned onto one of those miserable *picadas*. We bounced up and down into holes and ditches, across dried creeks, on granite and hard, sun-baked ground. Scarcely any game was seen and only a few signs of roan antelope. In the late afternoon we located the first so-called "control station," consisting of two mud-caked, primitive native huts. A few raucous hornbills and a solitary small gray monkey were our welcoming hosts.

The sepaio proved to be not only no help at all, but a definite liability. I saw some fresh lion tracks and soon after we heard the familiar roaring not far off in the bush. He was scared out of his wits. We stood around a while trying to decide whether to stay here or carry on farther. It was late afternoon. José cast some wary glances right and left, fixing his eyes anxiously on the only weapon, the Luger pistol. I felt that we would be safer within the truck than outside of it, and though we had not the vaguest idea how far we would have to drive before finding a better camping site, it was decided to push ahead. There was still enough daylight for us to travel a while longer.

We came upon a fairly open country and reached the second "control station." This was different from the first only in that it had four instead of two huts, no birds and no monkey, but a family of natives to greet us. Big and small, young and old were huddling over and around a little fire. They all were frightened because of the lions in the vicinity. They did not even have the usual stockade to protect them. Perhaps they had neither energy nor strength to build it. They all looked starved, sick, and listless.

It was a miserable situation, but we could not go farther that night. Our sepaio—that tower of police protection and the symbol of safety in khaki uniform with many brass buttons to decorate his tunic—by now was so terrified that his black color faded, blending in perfect camouflage with his uniform.

We made camp and soon had a big, blazing fire for protection close to the truck, took the pistol, and loaded it under many anxious eyes. Lions were everywhere, bold and obviously rarely molested.

José started to cook a supper. An old chap emerged at the smell of food from somewhere in the bush, came slowly, haltingly over to the fire, and, as natives do, stood silently and just watched. Gilchrist started a labored conversation in Umbundu and soon got him to the point where with the aid of a few cigarettes and a handful of sugar he thawed out.

"The lions and wild dogs kill many of the *palanca* here," said he placidly. "No gun, no protection, and no help of any kind. One of the women a fortnight ago was killed right here in the bush by them. The rest of her family moved far away," and his arm in an all-encompassing motion swept from one side to the other toward the Luando River. "Yes, we do have a few spears and a few bows and arrows"—showing a none too assuring, half-broken bow of his own—"but those are not enough. The sepaios are nowhere and even if they do come, they themselves are afraid." This remark did not need any more emphasis, as we judged from our own police boy.

Then he proceeded. "The bush from here on is thick. You could not go through with this car. The *picada* was just recently cut. Some strange white people were supposed to come here and were expected. Yes, the sepaios came first, collected all the folks around here, women, children, and old men, and we worked for many weeks to open and cut the bush. Who do you think those strange people could be? When will they come? How will they look?" A long silence, quizzical glances, and no more talk.

Again question after question slowly repeated, and finally the important clue was extracted. Yes, he knows where the *"palanca negra"* is, and yes, he is sure he speaks about the same *"palanca"* as the *senhores*. He is sure that they are the *sable* and not the *roan*. The Portuguese call the roan *"palanca"* also, but the giant sable is actually the *"palanca negra,"* meaning black roan. In view of these nuances one had to be very careful that the primitive brain and its meager knowledge of language would not mess up our effort. The next day early he would take us and though he could not promise it, he hoped he could show us a herd. Lately he had seen one.

"How many in the herd?"

That's difficult; he cannot count.

"Where are they?"

"Senhor, they are south of here and often come out to graze on a particular short grass much liked by them which is in bloom just now."

That was it. He must be right. I knew about that plant and the sable's liking for it. Now, if the lions were not chasing the herd, or killing some of them through the night, we might have luck.

Poking the fire, huddling close to it in the cold of the night, we talked and listened for a long while to the roar of lions, lapsing into silence as we gazed into the dying embers and dreamed of the giant sable. At last Gilchrist and I climbed into the truck, rolled into bedding, and kept the Luger close.

José woke up first; perhaps he did not sleep at all. It was bitter cold and he lay on the ground close to the fire. It was not only the warmest, but surely the safest place. Lions seemed to be circling us all that night. He tumbled and tossed at dawn until gradually everyone was roused. The sepaio was as helpless as ever; couldn't handle even an ax; didn't try or dare to go any distance into the bush to bring back wood for the fire. José and I went for it. With it we collected plenty of nettles and thorns in trousers and hands, and found some fresh lion tracks. There was a small pond with stagnant water and, though it looked harmless and enticing, I did not dare use the water from it. If rationed for two more days, I had sufficient water for cooking and drinking. It was evident and urgent that I locate the sables and get out of here in time. We did not tarry long and after a quick meal started out just about at daybreak.

I didn't mention to Sid Gilchrist that I had not spent the most peaceful night in the truck, and I am sure he felt the same way about it.

The sepaio I decided to take as a ballast, and only as a ballast. The old native holding onto his bow and spear climbed into the back with José while Sid and I settled down to the problem of driving. There was no path or clearance ahead. Shrubs and sparse tall grass dotted with gnarled, fantastically shaped, small trees and bushes blocked the way seemingly in every direction. The field was covered with hundreds of small and large anthills, hard-baked, leaden-colored clay structures looking like mushrooms, many ten to twelve inches in height and some as high as two to three feet. The white ant, "salale," a termite, builds these nests, invading anything, trees or bushes, it can devour. There are no giant anthills here like in Kenya or Tanganyika, or for that matter like in southern Angola. Around Andulo the natives chop out square blocks from such towering hills, honeycombed and hard as brick, and use them to build kilns for their primitive iron smelting.

Painfully slowly, bouncing continuously, bearing right, bearing left, often going in circles, we covered perhaps not more than a few kilometers when in the violet-hued haze ahead I noticed the faint silhouettes of some large animals. They looked like a mirage in the far distance, with the sun just rising above the horizon beyond them.

I stopped, lifted my Hensoldt field glasses and studied them for a long time, my shaking hands steadied against the door of the cab. José and the old guide came forward and soon we all were excited. Whether the group was small or large was indeterminable, but there against a grove of trees were those giant sables. I could hardly believe my eyes. My hands were still shaking and my heart was pounding. It was almost too easy, yet about a mile or so away the group stood serenely grazing and obviously not aware of us at all. I had to lay my plan carefully. I got my Bolex and checked the footage of film left in it, having about sixty more feet. I grabbed two more hundred-foot reels, gave them to José, who stuffed them into his army jacket. Sid had a Kodak 16-mm. movie camera with another couple hundred feet of film, so he, too, readied himself for action. We talked matters over and decided that while I stalked and filmed the sable, he would film me.

The old native, almost completely naked save for a piece of skin thrown diagonally over his hip, shivering in the cold of the early morning, followed with a crooked stick in his hand. A little wind blew from the side, so the stalk had to be in a line parallel with the sables' grazing direction. We had to make a mile-long detour in the bush, keeping hidden among the trees, to reach a point down-wind in line with them. Since they were out in the open not far from the edge of another small island of trees, I realized that when I got in line with them, my real difficulty in stalking would begin. From there I would have to crawl on my hands and knees for at least a good two hundred yards with nothing but a few small anthills to conceal me. But there was no other way. If I stayed in the bush and got above them, the wind blowing in the wrong direction would surely carry my scent and I would never see them again.

We walked as silently as four men can, among whom are two natives not much aware of the difficulties or problems of stalking. In the bush and in the dry season everything crackles. Bone-dry twigs and crisp leaves exploding like so many firecrackers can give enough warning to wake the dead. Many threatening, piercingly mad looks were directed at the careless natives and much grimacing and toe dancing went on before we finally reached our position. The woods jutted out in a triangle and on the edge were a few small-sized trees. From here on I had to go alone. I kicked up a bit of dust carefully and tested the air; wind hadn't changed.

First I looked over the entire group with glasses. I soon located a giant of the giants, an old jet-black bull with beautifully symmetrical, perfect horns curving back, almost reaching the center part of his spine. There he was, standing and watching his cows and many calves grazing in all directions. There were always one or two cows or young bulls keeping vigil with their heads held erect, attentive, alert, standing stock-still while the rest grazed. This was the rare

Puberty rites ceremony: symbolism—carrying the uninitiated young girl away from camp.   *Photo by De Sousa*

Puberty rites ceremony: the whipping scene.   *Photo by De Sousa*

Puberty rites ceremony at Gambos. The kneeling young girls' faces are covered for the first ten days after the operation. Coiffure is finished.

Photo by De Sousa

...es of young native women participating in the excision
...erty rites dance, with countless delicately woven bark
...celets on upper and lower arms, bark and bead necklaces,
...d decorations on hips and in hair. The ones with single
...al anklets have been initiated. The multiple bark anklets
...girls to the left signify that they are uninitiated.

Photo by De Sousa

...erty rites ceremony: the mask has been removed from the face; still the
...iated does not look up until she takes her final bath—a symbol of spiritual
...nsing.   *Photo by De Sousa*

At the end of the puberty rites ceremony, the girls leave camp and wash themselves as a symbol of starting a new existence and responsibilities.

Bushman woman and child carried in kaross. Note characteristic growth of hair in small islands or tufts.

The two brave lion hunters sat silently watching us with critical eyes.

Bushmen. Amused smiles as they hear their voices recorded on tape. Woman in foreground has safety pin in ear lobe.

Bushman hunter putting poison on his arrow tip.

The cubicle of the circumcised. Burning logs keep him warm throughout the night. There are ashes on the ground under him and his stripped bark skirt hangs above. In the rear are the two carved poles of male and female figures, symbolizing the union of the sexes.

Circumcised boys working at stripping bark for skirts. Bodies and faces are covered with ash.

Spirits dancing, late afternoon, at the Cheokwee circumcision camp. *Otamango* (the bird with the long beak) is in the rear.

Spirit dance at circumcision camp. Snow-white and jet-black.

Masked spirit dancers from the circumcision camp. *Sacalumbu,* "Terrific Jumper," and *Ofufuta,* "Swinging Tail."

cumcision camp: start of dance. *Namatumbu* with den mask and female stlike band across the t. *Otamango* (bells are at ed to his ankles) with ched grass mask.

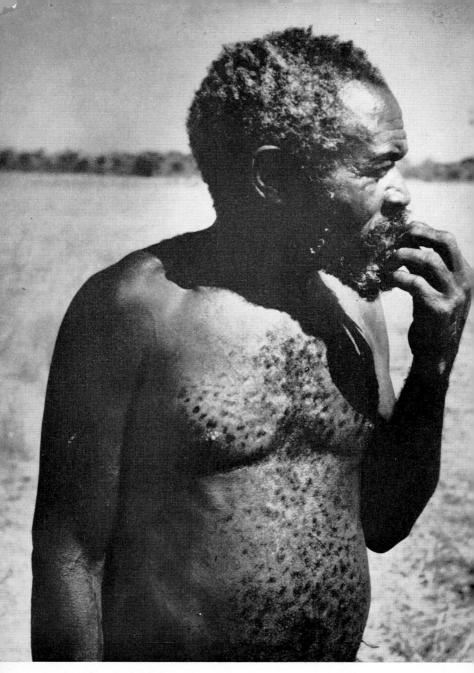

Balombo, the elephant hunter.

Quipungo funeral. The three diviners with rattles in hand start the mourning dance.

Quipungo funeral. Snow-white cowrie shells strung on a wide leather strap hang loosely directly over the spine—a sign of wealth. Shoulders of one are smeared with butter.

Quipungo funeral. Bereaved wives—hairdress stiffened with cow dung.
Photo by De Sousa

Quipungo funeral: mourners.

Quipungo funeral: the wives and relatives of the dead chief.

Quipungo funeral: log-beating ceremony.

Wrapped in black cloth, the crude coffin rests on two large boulders for the many days of ceremony. The three hired "wailing women" in background.

group I had dreamed of for so long and one day hoped to see.

Slowly I went down on my knees, camera in hand, while
the others stayed behind, hiding in back of tree trunks. Sid
started filming and I heard the burring of his camera as I
commenced to crawl out into the open. About fifty feet
straight ahead was a small anthill just tall enough to cover
me if I crawled on my stomach. There was a total of about a
hundred feet of open ground to cross in order to get close
enough to film the group. I knew that once I got to the anthill my chances for good pictures would be much more likely.

Prone and hardly moving at all, I wormed and wiggled
toward that anthill. At times it loomed like a mountain, and
then again as small as a mole mound. My mouth was dry as
cotton, eyes glued on them, heart pounding in my throat.
Each time a sable stopped grazing and looked up, I, too,
had to stop, absolutely stone-still. I had considerable trouble
masking the shiny, sun-reflecting parts of the camera where
here and there a narrow slit would catch the sun and act as a
sure giveaway even though I had taped most of it beforehand.
The old bull got suspicious and just as I was half crouching
on my knees, he started to look around, gazing straight at
me. I froze for minutes, not moving an eyelash. It seemed as
if hours passed before he started to graze again. Painfully I
realized that this was not a game for a man with rheumatism
in his joints. I creaked, ached, stiffened, and felt that I could
never move another foot forward, but, *but* I went on.

Scratching a bit of fine dust with my fingernails and letting
it blow lightly away, I tested the air again. Still all right. I
resumed the snail's pace, stretching both hands and camera
forward and pulling my body and legs after me. Suddenly

it occurred to me that I might meet a snake. The grass was short, but all the same, one thing I did not relish was to stare into a cobra, eye to eye. No flies, no bugs, and no ants (at least I didn't need to scratch, thanks to Providence), and that all helped as I slowly inched forward. I thought I would never reach that anthill.

To be sure of at least one shot at the sables, while lying there I slowly moved the camera forward close to my shoulder, got the group into the view finder, and started to film. The burring noise of the motor evidently could be heard. The cows became nervous and finally a dumb calf got inquisitive, left the group and headed toward the same anthill I had picked for myself. I stopped the motor; he seemed to change his mind—looking at me, he stopped too. I didn't dare take the camera from my face. I thought every muscle in my hands was paralyzed and my arms ached as if they had been pulled on a torture rack. He looked and looked as if trying to make up his mind about what he saw. Then he turned to go back and in a few yards began playing with another, so the frolicking got all the attention.

My chance came again. Once more I started inch by inch and progressed foot after foot till finally I reached the anthill. There, ducking my head, flattening myself, wishing I could shrink, I readied the camera again. The game was about one hundred feet away. The reddish color of the calves and cows was distinctly different from the soot-black and jet-black of the bulls.

I started to film, first with the three-inch telephoto, picking up details, and running off the entire sixty feet of film. So I had to reload. This was a major problem. It is so even

if one has all the cover, all the time, and unlimited sables
to view. Either the humming noise of the camera motor or
the motion of my body while cranking the camera made them
worried. They all stopped grazing and as one, the whole
group, exactly fourteen, stood as though cast in bronze, looking in my direction. I ceased cranking and remained motionless. We stared at each other for moments, no, for minutes.
It felt like hours. The wind was in my favor and all I needed
was a chance to get the new reel in the camera. It was some
job. The cover plate comes off easily, but the spool must be
removed to thread in new film. Every second seemed to be
hours and my nervous hands, like clumsy tools, refused to
operate. I missed the sprockets, had to start again. I finally
succeeded and got it reloaded. A few young bulls, fully
grown and mature but with not much length to their otherwise impressive horns, started to fight, a made-to-order scene
for any wild-game photographer. The whole sequence was
filmed and I turned the camera on the grand old man. There
he was, watching his young fighting for supremacy.

Keeping my eyes on him, I slowly rolled over on my side
and, while shielding with my body the field glasses and the
camera's reflecting parts, gradually inched toward him.
There he was, an aggressive and dangerous antelope who, if
he should take a notion to, could pick me up on his beautiful
curved horns. Here was the grand monarch all by himself.

For years I have been familiar with the extreme inquis-
itiveness of the caribou or deer in the northern woods. I often
shot or filmed them by whistling or taking out a red handkerchief and dangling it up and down. They invariably will stop
if they do not get your scent, and often even turn back,

prance, and circle around you just to see who you are or what you are doing.

I had to do something, something desperate, and hope that the sable would respond like a caribou might.

I stood up full length suddenly, positioned the camera high at shoulder and fixed to my eyes, with arms steady as possible, step by step, slowly, deliberately I advanced toward the group. That tremendous bull watched me come. I sensed that he was trying to figure out what this strange apparition could be. The first moment they all stood silent, gazing at a curious new sight. With pounding heart and shaking hands I filmed about twenty to thirty feet, recranked the camera slowly without letting my arm down and walked closer. They stood their ground and I filmed again.

Now the big bull started. He trotted a few steps toward me, looming awfully big in the view finder while I kept filming. Then a cow approached and I walked a few steps closer. They were almost incredible, this rare, wonderful group of giant sables, sweeping black horns sixty inches or over in length, jet-black bodies close to six feet high at the withers, sharply slanting rear quarters, snow-white manes on top of and beneath the necks of the bulls, surrounded by rust-colored calves. I could be no more now than thirty feet away; I could smell their pungent odor. The wind was still blowing from them to me. At close range I filmed again.

The spell was broken.

Up leaped the big bull, kicked and snorted like a horse. The band joined the leader, jumped and pranced wildly away. God knows why I wasn't trampled! Sables all around me, I obstinately filmed, frozen in excitement, though my eyes, arms, and fingers ached, until I reached the end of the reel.

In the dust stirred by thudding, thumping, and stampeding feet the vanishing sight of a noble animal faded away.

Chapter XIV

THE CIRCUMCISION

T HE DRUMS were beating again. They were here, they were there, on the ridges far away, in the bush close by, but they were all over, filling the silent air of the night, filling it with the steady beat of the drums. A message went across, a call, a strange, mystic invitation to the weird rite. A note was given to be spread in the night to all the ones who know, to all who are a part of an age-old ritual . . . initiation.

I must find the place. Where are those strange people of the bush, those Cheokwees? Like animals they withdrew into the deep, almost impenetrable jungle to hide and to protect themselves and their worshipings from the spying, from the critical eyes of the white—missionaries, authorities alike.

Is it wisdom to oppress it? Who knows? I must see what they do.

The drums are beating.

Circumcision camps are not built every year and are far apart, concealed, hidden in the jungle or bush so that only the "Knowing Ones" can find them.

An old man, old as a gnarled tree, half Christian, half heathen, an outcast from his society, and still a member of the sect. The key to the lock, if only willing—I must find *him* first. He lived somewhere nearby, this man who knew and if willing could remember where to go.

It took a long time to find his place. Endless breaking through jungle undergrowth finally forced me to give up driving farther and leave the truck to proceed on foot. Two native boys were the guides and after hours of trudging we finally came upon the old man's hut, well hidden in the bush. He came out haltingly from a grass-thatched shed, putting his arms across his chest, head bending down, and then, clapping several times with the palms of his hands, welcomed us. Years before, a daughter of his was helped—difficult labor; she almost lost her life. Here he was, humble and subservient, yet impressive, appealing, and dignified beyond description.

We talked to him. Hesitant as he was, it looked like a toss-up whether he would agree. How much, if any, power, how much trust could he command at the circumcision camp? I wondered. But I kept on asking him to come and help; persuasion and his obligation perhaps—because of his daughter —finally made him agree to join. After picking up his bundle and a crooked walking stick he started to lead us farther into the bush.

We tramped among small and large thornbushes, treading amid anthills, jumping across fallen, rotted logs for a long, long time, then came upon a small clearing. The trees here were chopped, showing signs of fresh work on them, to a remaining height of two-three feet. The stumps looked like so many sore fingers everywhere. The native all over Africa chops trees down in this manner, either because the blade of his ax, fitted into a knoblike handle, is better suited to work high above ground, or because when he burns the ground over later, he can extricate stumps and roots more easily. Or perhaps simply because he is too lazy to bend down farther from the waist.

This circle, about three to four hundred feet in diameter, was so well hidden in the tangle of bush that unless the path leading to it were known, one could pass by and never find it. I have often seen large, cleared areas, full of chopped-down trees, but a single one, untouched, left standing like a sentinel, and I often wondered just why *one* tree was left behind. A tree stood on this clearing, too.

It is the universal belief of all primitives that every living thing has a spirit, so, to avoid angering the spirits of the trees, they always leave at least one standing. This acts as a host to the spirits of all the fallen trees, and as long as they have a place to congregate and make themselves comfortable there, they are pacified and not too ired by the poor mortals who have cut the rest of them.

Before me was this clearing and the solitary tree. From the distance came faint drumming and incantation mixed at times with high-pitched, childish, shrill voices.

Could this mean that we had come upon an unusual act here? I looked at my old man. He must have known the exact time of this program. He *had* come through. The stolid face showed no expectation. He motioned to follow and just kept on walking. But the boys did not, and refused to go farther. No amount of coaxing could induce them to proceed. It was peculiar. Finally I had to take over the camera and film packs they were carrying, and then followed him alone. As I looked back, they were sitting down making themselves comfortable and evidently settling for a long wait. I could not understand this then, but later discovered that the reason for this reluctance was that they were worried, in spite of my presence, about being forcefully held at this camp and circumcised. They were fearful, not being members of this "noble brotherhood," of an adverse reaction from the spirits hovering above the camp, and of being circumcised, or perhaps receiving a beating from the members of the sect for no special reason. It is not an infrequent occurrence and can happen to any male strayed or lost near such a camp. This surely would be little appreciated by them. Little did I think about my own chances among such overzealous primitives!

I noticed two small, square, blocklike objects, honeycombed clay and gray in color, cut out of anthills, each just flat and wide enough to permit sitting on them. They looked like stools seen in front of huts in any native village. One of the blocks was adjacent to a tree trunk and the other was in a line about two feet away from the first.

While I was looking this over, a strange procession emerged from the bush. Five older men slowly dancing back and forth, carrying a small boy, limp, and evidently doped, from the effect of some concoction. Five other young boys followed. They all sang in strange, high-pitched voices while dancing to the rhythm of two drums. They acted as though in a trance.

I thought an act of circumcision might be starting here since I knew it took place after days of dancing and invoking the spirits, during which time the boys were given a concoction to make them drug-happy for the particular occasion. I got camera ready and started to film.

A strangely garbed, weird-looking man, face painted with

brilliant yellow, red, and blue stripes around the eyes and mouth, looking like a Chinese dragon, sat down carefully on the first block nearest to the tree, braced his body firmly against the trunk, and held the naked youngster between his legs. The boy, limp and head bobbing up and down, faced the operator, who was sitting on the second block. He had a head-dress like a gigantic bird with a curved beak bending over his forehead and he, too, was painted with bright colors. And now, amid constant chanting with the increased staccato of the drums, with a quick, circular motion, using a very sharp, triangular iron piece, he cut the foreskin. The result was gratifying to all concerned since a tremendous howling by all followed and more dancing went on.

The boy, sufficiently doped to look upon the detached skin with a "detached" feeling, expressed little interest in all this. The small part of his anatomy so forcefully and ably sepa-rated from the rest of him was buried right away in a small clump of dirt close to the tree by another, dressed equally ferociously for *this* occasion. The next in line went on the operating table. In quick succession the entire group of six candidates was circumcised in less than one hour.

Each circumcised was treated with an astringent fluid pre-pared by the medicine man and the elders, *sekulus,* belong-ing to the "Order of the Circumcised." No one is allowed either to view or be a part of this ritual unless he himself has been circumcised. What had happened? Why was I allowed to be here and how could I get away after viewing all this? I looked for an answer, or at least for reassurance. My native just stood at my side, motionless, silent, unperturbed. Who is this man? What signals, if any, did he give to the ones here that I was accepted? I don't know. I still don't know even now. Certainly I saw no exchange of signs, neither did I hear words spoken, yet I know that all noticed our presence, and especially *my* presence, but no one paid any attention.

A bandage comprised of leaves and twines was placed on the wound and some wood ash thrown on it to prevent bleeding. If by our standards this procedure was not as medically reassuring as one is accustomed to, still I did not see a single boy bleed much. And so the boys were carried away amid more chanting and dancing into the circumcision camp.

The sun dropped behind the horizon and suddenly it was dark. There was little or nothing more to do here. I turned back and reached the old guide's hut after a while. There I stayed for the night, pondering about my unusual luck. I now had no doubt that through sheer good fortune this old man I had met, not only knew all that was going on in this forest, but, too, had the unquestionable authority to command respect and so I was allowed to see everything.

Early next morning with films and camera I started on the winding path again and returned to the camp of the circumcised. I was not questioned by either spirits or mortals, and entered the stockaded area. Planks made from freshly cut trees ten to fifteen feet in height were closely tied to each other, driven deep into the ground. So thickly were they shielded by the branches and leaves that it was impossible to look through them. The cleverly arranged outward-leaning angle of them precluded the possibility of climbing up. It could be entered only through an opening facing east and just wide enough to allow a body to squeeze through. Fourteen boys widely differing in body build and height, some almost degenerate-looking with protruding stomachs and rickety, curved legs, were there. Spindly, emaciated bodies, covered from head to toe with gray ash producing a ghostly look, were working here, stripping bark from logs. Some were drying it and others weaving it into skirts.

In the background was a fascinating row of double pole carvings each about four feet above ground, freshly debarked and shining. The *usamba* tree is used for this only and its red string bark fiber was used to make the short skirt for the circumcised boy. These poles in juxtaposition had primitive carvings of a head on top, one representing a male and the other a female, distinguishable because of the difference in hair dressing and skull formation. To the circumcised, adolescent boys these represent the symbols of unification of both sexes. Each of the double totem-polelike stakes was directly in line but behind an oval-shaped cubicle, single and double, all with a narrow entrance, four feet in height, and without a roof.

A few of the boys lay in this specially prepared place built of debarked sticks arranged vertically in "U" shape. The ground was thickly strewn with gray wood ash and a log placed where the head rests, acting as a pillow under the neck. A crude, twined, bark-laced hoop, oval in shape and both ends windowed into the size and shape of the upper thighs through which both legs were inserted, protected the wound effectively. There they lay for the first few days with this hoop strapped to the upper thighs. Each boy, himself, prior to this operation makes his own hoop and later, when he is able to move around the camp during the day, he hangs this in front of his little cubicle. A fire was burning on both sides of each little stockade to keep the entirely naked boy warm through the night. Water and food are brought to him for the first few days. Every time a boy was fed, a small amount of the food was given as a sacrifice to the ancestral spirits by placing it on a special altar located centrally in the camp at the rear.

They got up in a line, started to chant, and an elderly man sitting, holding between his knees a small hand-zither-like instrument over a halved gourd, which acted as a sounding board, played with them in unison.

Soon a short, stocky chap, either the medicine man or one of his assistants, gave some kind of command, to me sounding like a vigorous mouth gargling. All boys stopped, got up, and walked in single file into a segregated area. There was a long log stripped of its bark. On that they sat down facing another man who carried in a large gourd a reddish-colored, rolled-up twine ball immersed in a yellow liquid. It was some kind of tannic-acid solution and must have been an astringent. He went from boy to boy and carefully squeezed over each wound this saturated twine from which the fluid oozed out onto the exposed part.

Early in the morning and in the afternoon during the first fourteen days following the circumcision this is performed regularly. How many times will those wounds get infected? I hesitated to test my welcome here, but was anxious to see the wounds, turned to my "mentor" and tried to explain this as best I could. He talked to the others and motioned to me to go ahead. So I bent and looked a few over quickly, noticed no pus and only a little swelling. The dressings were applied cleverly, utilizing a particular species of tree leaves rolled around and secured under and over with twine fastened around the wound. This stayed comfortably and sufficiently attached so that while they jumped around, sat, got up, lay down, it did not interfere with activities in the least.

During all this the medicine man turned his head continually, looking around. His three assistants every so often darted suddenly outside the stockade, emitting bloodcurdling yells and running like maniacs. Occasionally a woman, either the mother, sister, or another relative of a boy within the camp, might come and try to peek through to see what is going on inside. If they are caught, they are beaten up, and in addition are forced to pay a sacrifice such as a fowl or a goat. It is a high price to pay for such curiosity. This is then offered to the spirits of the camp, but eaten up by the medicine man and his assistants.

If difference or strife arises among the boys, fights seldom, if ever, break out. I witnessed an effective method of punishment. The issue was evaded when I asked what the boy did, and I could not pry further. I saw, however, the offender being grabbed and carried by four other boys outside to a nearby brook. There he was placed into the cold water up to his neck. It's a really effective method.

Late in the afternoon some of the boys started to dress three of the older men who were garbed in fine grass netlike suits fitting the body tightly. Strange headdresses and masks were donned. A large female breastlike attachment was fixed to the chest of one, to the merriment of all boys. He was the *Namatumbu*. The other, who was the *Otamango*, had bells attached to his ankles. The third had a fantastic-looking long tail, swaying back and forth; he was the *Ofufuta*. Later a fourth one, a veritable acrobat, joined them executing tremendous leaps in all directions. They called him the *Sacalumbu* (Terrific Jumper). They all belonged to the Male Secret Society.

The boys themselves, covered with silvery-gray ash, looked like so many gnomes adorning strange gods from a distant land. Amid chanting the "spirits" left the camp and disappeared in the thick bush.

Soon from the distant village women started to chant. I left the camp and crossed the low bush, following a narrow path. As I neared the village from the east and the parallel rays of the setting sun threw a golden-reddish color on everything, I came upon the grotesquely dressed dancing figures representing the spirits *(Ovinganji)*. *Otamango* like a prehistoric bird with a long, curved beak; *Sacalumbu* like a demon loose from the depths of hell; *Ofufuta* with his swinging tail, leaping into the air like a vulture; and *Namatumbu* with an outlandish female body configuration. Slowly, shyly, yet deliberately they emerged from the bush with light, dancing steps, coming closer and retreating again as though uncertain how far to approach. Intermittently, with cacophonous shrieks, they swung back and forth toward the women bunched into a tight, frightened group.

Then the drums started and as the tempo increased the weird figures moved faster in united rhythmic gyration. The tinkling bells on the ankles of the *Otamango* blended into the drum tones. Their accelerating, weird cries reverberated like a deep bass as the circling dancers whirled faster and faster. More of the "spirits" joined in, flinging themselves around in frenzy and spellbinding the onlookers to the point where the singing, crying, drumming and everything else became a kaleidoscope of primitive fear, desire, and faith.

The sun went down, the "spirits" dispersed, but the weird cries were still echoing and re-echoing from the distant bush and the heavy pall of mysticism enveloped everything.

It was a typical manifestation of a closely woven society performing its rituals and ceremonies according to the laws of centuries. From the very outset this occasion so deeply impresses the young who undergo the tangible act of initiation that it produces a solidarity of cause. From that moment he is one of them; he is a member of a fraternity in which his actions will be judged by his associates, and wherein solidarity, dignity, and responsibility are taught by the sponsors and the elders who are members of the same clan. How can one fail to appreciate this intricate mechanism and its beneficial effect on the initiated?

How evident is the salutary effect of discipline, acting in unison, sharing responsibility, and working together. It is the basic purpose for the boys to remain in camp for a designated period. The circumcision itself must be visible indication to the rest of the tribe that they now are candidates for special training. They are preparing themselves for new roles in tribal life.

Actually the African native lives by stages. The *first*, from birth until two years of age, is known as the "spiritless stage." The *second* stage begins when the spirit enters into him, and this, according to the native's belief, is when the toddler shows some intelligence and power of reasoning.

The child is accepted as the possessor of a spirit from here on. He or she in this similar age group, and with older boys and girls, will learn about flowers, trees, animals, snakes, ants, bees, et cetera. If they are members of a nomadic and cattle-breeding tribe, they will follow the herd of goats, sheep, or cattle. They will learn during these years a few simple methods of trapping and hunting, songs and dances, and play games, primitive as they are. During this stage both sexes are involved in *common* pursuits. Here and there a girl might be placed with her elder sister and in close association with the womenfolk of the tribe in order to assist with chores such as carrying water in gourds, learning how to weave baskets, helping with the cooking, and watching over the smaller children.

When they reach the preadolescent age, they are in the *third* stage. The communal singing and dancing are dominating from here on. They are now separated. Each sex gradually assumes more responsibility. If they are boys, they will stay away from the village for days and weeks, following cattle, protecting it from marauding animals. They forge or make their bows, arrows, and spears under the guidance of elders, and learn how to handle them. If they are girls, they are tilling the fields and taking over the duties of housekeeping, and by now are capable of cooking.

Life really becomes serious, however, when they are honored by being selected to join the group for circumcision and, if girls, for the puberty rites ceremony. In this *fourth* stage they are confined to a camp. They undergo the operation and the subsequent training, discipline, communal hunting or working, singing, and making sacrifices to the spirits. This welds them together into a unit that parallels a fraternity. They learn to be proud to belong to a common group and every member thereof in his behavior is responsible to every other member of this society. They are under the supervision and tutelage of sponsors who in turn have undergone the same operation and identical training years before. Only with each other and their sponsors can they freely communicate, exchange ideas, and discuss matters during this time. And so a decided caste system develops in which the young native lives and grows, bearing the indelible mark of mutual responsibility toward his own group. It is acting on this premise individually that keeps them collectively within the dictates of their age-old laws and the do's and don't's of their tribal system.

The boys stay within those stockaded camps four to six weeks and the girls as long as two or more months, both learning much about sex life and future responsibilities. Still a few years must elapse before they are ready for marriage. Whether or not they indulge in cohabitation during this interim depends on the relative strictness of the tribe.

The metamorphosis in morals—evident in this modern age —has been noted in Africa too.

The operation itself on both sexes is significant now only as a continuance of bygone requirements of a much stricter tribal existence. Consequently the self-respect and dignity this ceremony instilled within the group in its more meaningful days are now lacking and the restrictions of sex life, therefore, are vastly relaxed.

The *fifth* stage while growing into man and womanhood is spent by males in hut and village building, participating in hunts and trapping, and by the young women in cooking, supervising children, and generally helping their family and others within the village.

The *sixth* stage is entered when marriage occurs. The man, when he pays for his first wife with so many goats, oxen, or both, becomes established as a member of the junior group of elders. As soon as his wife bears him a child, he automatically enters the succeeding stage. He is then regarded as one of the most important members of village life. His opinion is sought after, listened to, and in fact required to be stated in village matters involving illness, death, dances, moving the village, and so on.

The *final* stage is reached when the native becomes an elder of the village, the most venerable and respected member of the tribe. He or she, as the case may be, then decides on many vital issues and those decisions are always law unto themselves. Until the end of the nineteenth century only elders were allowed to drink to the point of getting drunk. If a younger man or woman before this final stage ever became drunk, it meant ostracism. If on any occasion throughout their lives a man or woman committed a wrong by displaying greed, stealing, or killing anyone without permissible and justifiable cause, his own contemporaries in the group to which the culprit belonged were the severest jurors and judge. He would be ostracized as though blackballed from a country club in modern society.

In the eye of a native nothing could be harsher punishment than exile.

This skillful and perfectly balanced system, like a smooth and compact ball with its inherent cohesive qualities, enabled the native by his own standard to exist on a fine ethical and moral level. Only in rare instances did those well-regulated tribes have trouble among themselves. The white man's civilization removed a very, if not the most, important restraining factor in his life. It did impede to a certain extent the functioning of the tribal system, particularly when those circumcision and excision ceremonies were discouraged, frowned upon, and often eliminated.

So this intricately intertwined and tightly woven ball has unraveled and the loose ends are now flying in all directions. Who can ever hope to tie it together again?

Chapter XV

THE LEOPARD

I HAPPENED to come upon them here in the bush.
Both were scared, ready to run. With a visible jerk, a loud
heave, and silent resignation I came to a halt. I knew I was
lost and that by now was a common occurrence. There was
no use in asking them where to go; I could not talk to them.
There they stood, timid, questioning, and ready to spring,
like scared animals.

I saw a terribly mangled arm loosely hanging and rolled
into an ocher-dyed blanket carried after a fashion on the
thin, emaciated body of one of them. What is this? How
can a man stand there, stolid, impassive, and holding with
his left hand onto that bleeding, mangled right arm to steady
it? What happened? José came forward and a timid, halting,
difficult conversation ensued. The dialect was like a barking
animal, short, rapid, staccato, and in disjointed syllables.
Even my ear could tell that the language was different.

Something finally was understood. An animal had mauled
him. How and where did it happen? Where were they heading? What was he trying to do with that helpless, pitiful-
looking arm? They had spears in hand and short, wicked-
looking, wide-bladed knives hanging on braided, finger-thick

leather-cord belts. Save for a small leather apron over and across their loins they were naked beneath those blankets.

I took out a medical kit and tried to indicate that I might be able to help if allowed to take a look. No, they would have none of that. Both of them, with an animal-like distrust, instantly drew back. I tried to tell José to reassure him. That was in vain. So the next best thing I could offer was to put them into the back of the truck and drive them wherever they wanted to go. After a long hesitation, sign language and persuasion, gifts of food, sugar, salt, and then cigarettes I convinced them that I meant no harm. So they did climb up into the truck with José and we started moving.

It was a strange, fearful, and almost foreboding country. Did it really hold a secret danger, or did it just seem that way because I was lost and for days everything looked suspicious? Maps were absolutely no use. I had brought them along from the States. They were aerial surveys, inaccurate, poorly marked, and insufficiently defined, more confusing than helpful. On this occasion I had gotten onto some small path that had branched off days before, and now again, following the wrong lead, I gave up and had to go by compass. Fuel I had in a drum and, according to calculations, I must soon hit the river. From there on a grassland—at least on the map—an open grassland was ahead of me. And then a small town or settlement somewhere in the vicinity of about a day's travel. On roadless but flat country I usually used a gallon for ten miles, so with my extra fifty gallons of gas I had more than enough. Though by now I mistrusted my logistics and maps thoroughly, even so, the distance I had to cover could be no more than 200 miles in all. Because of small swamps here and there I took many detours and in one place simply could not get through the bush, so I went at least fifty miles around and now here I was, and lost again.

This is, and I knew it, the wildest and most isolated spot in Angola. White men disappear here and never come back. I stayed just a week ago not far north from here with a Boer farmer, an old, old man with a gnarled, toughened body like those African acacias, with a dirty, mustard-colored beard flowing down onto his chest. One night as I asked him, he spoke like a voice from a musty barrel. "Ja, Doktor, dees iz strange landt, very strange!"

Here, fierce, small tribes wander back and forth in the bush, still cannibals.

"I und da Cheokwees are trading mit dem. Dey bring me skins, skins of giant snakes und furs of rare monkeys. I am giving dem salt, Doktor."

So here I was, with these two men, one so badly chewed up, and heading God knows where. I had driven a few miles when they started to bang frantically from behind. I stopped; they and José climbed out. It seemed they wanted to go in a different direction. It always puzzled me how any one of them could tell *what* direction to go by just looking out from a canvas-covered rear of a truck and, too, looking at everything from the back, when I could never tell where I was going, looking ahead and seeing in all directions, wide and far away.

Strange people, strange land.

One got on the hood of the truck to lead in this trackless,

very rough country. From here on I changed direction frequently. They knew the country and knew how to take me through the bush. So I drove on.

I grew more and more apprehensive. I remembered my old Boer. My guns I had with me and if I got into a tough spot, I could shoot my way out perhaps—perhaps. But I did not relish it.

I didn't drive long. Suddenly I found myself surrounded by very unfriendly-looking, naked, but armed savages. They sprang out from nowhere, each had a spear similar to the ones carried by the men I had picked up, and the same kind of vicious-looking knives at their sides. Obviously they belonged to the same tribe. I stopped and my two friends (were they friends?) got into a long conversation with them. Not too reassuring glances were thrown toward me, but I acted unconcerned and tried to save the situation, just waiting. Something finally was decided, perhaps in my favor. Now all tried to climb up on the truck. That even a jeep truck could not stand, so I got half a dozen packed into the rear and quite a few of my friends on the fenders, on the hood, and all over. The rest of them were running beside the truck. So a friendly contact was established.

Shortly we reached a village. It was primitive and stockaded with clusters of huts within. I got out and walked up, following the band and the man with the lacerated arm. The hard-packed, dusty ground looked like a heaven for a garbage collector. Discarded, broken gourds, denuded cobs of maize, and sun-bleached bones or animal carcasses were all over. A few emaciated, sour-looking dogs were loitering around. A dismal scene.

Jabbering, an old woman came forth and, like an expert, without much hesitation inspected the mangled limb, mumbled back and forth, looked around, and gave some directions to the few standing around who were watching this palaver intently.

She disappeared inside a hut for a while and soon came out with a gourd containing some dirty-looking liquid, water or such, and a bag. The old wizard got busy after a short discussion evidently concerning the relative merits of the case and the fee to be paid later. I just stood by and watched her do her tricks.

She sat down and so did the man, facing her. With a monotone singsong, almost like an incantation, she shook everything out of the bag. Out fell dried bones, curled-up skins, small pieces, little pebbles, and heaven knows what. These were the sacred tools of her trade. She was a medicine woman.

She got up, walked around in a small circle, and gazed intently toward the middle, where all those strange-looking objects were lying in a disorderly heap. Like an old vulture, her head covered with a dirty shawl, she threw evil glances in all directions. The men stood around in a cluster and watched her in awe. Then she laid the man down, took a little fat, and smeared it over the gashed wounds. The victim either had a good deal of self-control, or faith in her doings. At any rate torn muscles and shreds of skin were put back in haphazard fashion into a bloody mass without a single indication of pain or discomfort. It was some neat surgery mixed with a judicious amount of psychosomatic approach! Incidentally I never remember seeing a native faint.

The best part of this *à l'Afrique* method of plastic surgery came when she took out from a square wooden box about a dozen or more long thorns, no doubt collected and kept for just such purpose. They were the usual thorns I so often have seen on the whistle-thorn trees, an acacia of smaller growth. They were about an inch long, slender, and extremely sharp-pointed. How often I cussed getting close to them and finding myself neatly spiked by those very sharp points in spite of my thick leather jacket.

She pierced flesh and skin with those, and then hooked each end with a knife into a barb, like a fishhook, and so both ends, barbed and hooked, facing each other kept the wound's edges neatly together. When she finished the job, it would have been a credit to any surgeon in any modern hospital. A little ash and much dirt were thrown on for good measure, and, to facilitate healing, she spat on it three times. There was more talk, more grinning, and more spitting, and the deal was closed to the satisfaction of all concerned.

She grabbed all her displayed objects, carefully put them back into the bag, and left with dignity, not even casting a glance at me. I was amazed. I had heard and read that in some part of the world natives deliberately break off the head of some large ant and use its claws for holding wounds together, but I never dreamed that thorns, too, could be made into such efficient clips as those.

The "patient" got up in a very matter-of-fact manner and everything seemed to be under control. I tried to get some help first in finding the river. I couldn't understand them and they couldn't understand me. At any rate my chums were helpful enough to be willing to come along. They got into the truck with me again and went back pretty much along the same route I had come.

After bouncing up and down we arrived at another village. They belonged here, and I found the answer to the chewed-up arm. A man-eating leopard was on the rampage. Everyone was frightened and helpless. They all came up to greet me. Just the night before a child had been killed and in the fight to chase the vicious cat away this native got badly mangled. I looked over the kraal carefully into which the leopard had entered the previous night. Nothing much was disturbed. He had crawled through a loose plank in the side. It was a very small opening, considering how large and heavy he must be, from his pug marks left behind in the fine dust. So here was the story. He terrorized this entire village, stole and killed a few dogs for weeks before, then killed a child. Everyone asked me to stay.

Among the five most dangerous game of Africa, leopard, elephant, rhino, lion, and buffalo, the leopard is the smallest in size, and seldom turns into a man-eater. Yet he is cunning, clever, and a stealthy cat, ugly, bloodthirsty and unpredictable. Once wounded, he is the most formidable of all. The lion will at least give you a chance. Either he will roar before he attacks, or will roar evenings and all night when he is on a hunt to kill. You know where he is. Often he will come at you in the daytime and, yes, sometimes at night, but at least you know about his intentions. Not so with the leopard. No, he will steal away a child practically from the arms of its mother, a woman from her hut. Once he becomes a man-eater, he is ten times as bad as any lion can be. He will always attack, steal you, and kill you at night.

Years ago natives often left their dead in large baobab trees. These have deep and hollow cavities in their trunks, too convenient to overlook as a place for depositing a corpse. Hyenas and leopards will be attracted as undertakers.

In Tanganyika I saw about a hundred-pound wart hog killed practically under my eyes and dragged, hoisted up in a tree by one of them. That is the way a leopard does. A cunning and sly, ferocious beast, figuring and thinking out everything in advance. If he makes his own kill, to prevent the hyenas, jackals, or even the lions from stealing it away, he takes it up ten to fifteen feet high onto a tree and wedges it between the branches just to come back night after night to feed on it.

This very habit helps to locate and kill him, for otherwise it is almost impossible to stalk or hunt him. He is elusive, sleeps during the day in thick, impenetrable bush country or in a tree, and hunts by night only. Unless one just happens to meet him, usually one can seldom find him. Putting a bait, a kill, on a tree in the right location will invariably attract him sooner or later, so one might have a chance to get a shot at him.

I decided to stay and try for him.

The day was almost over and I had no time left before sunset to locate anything to kill for bait, so I settled down and went to bed in the truck. The frightened people kept large fires going here and there all night and one could hear those monotoned, low-pitched, jabbering voices while the stars shone above.

Nothing happened through that night.

I got out early the next day. Not far from the village I shot a wart hog and decided just to let it lie where it fell. Early in the afternoon I went back and noticed that there were practically no vultures on it. A few circled around but never lighted on the carcass, or they waited in nearby trees, as one sees them do in Central East Africa. There my wart hog would have been eaten and nothing but white bones left after a few hours. I selected a likely section close to a creek where the trees were sparse on both banks and dragged the wart hog there by truck over a good half mile of stumps, bush, grass, and hills. Then we hoisted it up and tied it into the crotch of a small baobab tree.

I left the place and did not come back until the next night. No signs of feeding on it; nothing touched it; I decided to stay out there until dark. As the sun set and from the distance came the throbbing sounds of drums, it made me feel very, very lonely being all by myself, no white, no one to talk to, and here now for days on this merry chase. What if this ugly cat of the devil right now is watching me, figuring how to jump at me, instead of my getting the jump on him? It was not pleasant.

Nothing happened. I was relieved when it was dark enough so that I could not see any way to find an excuse to start back for camp. I inspected the country carefully next morning again. There were few rocky areas, *kopjes*, and though the grass was not yet burned, and the bush was fairly high, with the exception of a few acacias and baobabs, everything was pretty open and would give me a chance to look over far away in all directions with glasses and watch what was going on. I would not need to approach the tree until sure that he was on it. I knew that, cunning as he is, the leopard is intensely local in habits and will not stray away from an area in which he is hunting. So it will be a matter of time and perseverance. They seldom take over each other's territory and never hunt together as lions will.

Now there was not much to do but wait and play the game accordingly. That night, while sitting in front of my fire listening to the jackals and weird, chilling laughs of the hyenas, I tried to figure out what my leopard might do. Would he come and try to make another killing at the village, finish off another child, or dog, or goat? Or would he take the easy way out and come to feed on my bait?

There were humans here, primitive humans, all frightened and some killed and in danger all the time. This had to be my show from here on. I was lonely, but I would stay. Here I was, stuck with or because of my own decision. This is bad. After all, one can always find an excuse for someone else's decision, but never should do so for his own. I knew too well that even if I stayed all night and every night close to one or another kraal, chances of his bungling into the hut near me were almost nil. So I decided to stay in the truck. José liked it better.

And so another night went by and as soon as the sun came up and there was sufficient light to see, I went again to inspect the bait.

I had visited my kill up till now daily at dawn and again around sunset and stopped always a few hundred yards away, approaching the tree according to the prevailing wind, but keeping downwind. I looked the tree over very, very carefully each time, examined its branches and watched for every telling mark with glasses. I knew well that if he were close, I would find him either directly on the same tree and perhaps on the bait, or maybe on another neighboring tree, stretched out full length on a limb, covered, blended in between the lights and shadows with his golden yellow body and square, rosetted black spots camouflaged.

No luck. He hadn't even touched the kill. But neither did he show up in the village.

By now I had spent five days more here than I bargained for. Yet the longer I stayed, the more I felt I could not leave. Simple, helpless, frightened souls! In the mornings one or two women would come with ground maize and a few eggs, offering them on their outstretched palms as a token of appreciation for assurance and safety. I stayed. At least I thought one more day would make no difference.

On the sixth day, early as I drove out again and stopped the truck to look and listen, I noticed nothing unusual. I kept the glasses for a long while glued to my eyes, but no —nothing. The bait by now was so well known to me and to the boys that even if a small branch or leaf had been disturbed, we would have noticed it. I watched the native who guided me every day and sat by my side. He with a wry smile tried to say, "Nothing doing." I wondered if his better eyesight had detected something I failed to see. No—he just smiled back again. "Nothing doing." So I drove on slowly and headed toward the tree. I wanted to see in what condition the kill was. I was almost directly under it and leaning out of the cab slightly in order to look upward. Suddenly I saw like a yellow streak with lightning speed, the leopard jumping directly from above and silently disappearing in the nearby bush.

So he had been there and right under my nose!

How could that happen? Where were my eyes? What did I do? How could I miss such a large, yellow, black-spotted cat? How could this have happened? I with glasses, powerful glasses, and the natives, not one but three, with eyes straining, and we all were fooled. I could cry. Anger and disappointment, frustration, six days of effort, gone with the wind! All this just because I was not cautious enough, because I did not look longer. But God Almighty, how could one look longer or more? How could one be more cautious? I was boiling mad and dumfounded.

I did not get out of the truck. At least I had sense enough to remember that as long as I stayed in it I would leave no scent anywhere. I drove around closer to the tree from the other side and saw that my pig on the tree was well chewed up. Much of the guts and entrails had been devoured, so he had a feast all right. I just stayed there in the car and, as though half paralyzed, couldn't think, had nothing to plan for the time being. I swore and swore and swore again. How utterly stupid of me! And then I heard a jackal barking, a persistent, high-pitched, angry bark. It was a heaven-sent good sign. This small, alert animal of the bush, the only one who can claim friendship with a lion, the only one who is allowed to get close to a kill while he feeds on it, was upset and gave notice of it. The leopard must still be close. He had not left the bush and my jackal knew it, maybe right now was still seeing him. This big, man-eating cat must be slinking somewhere under the thick bush close by. The jackal kept on barking. This leopard, *my* leopard, still must

be close. I didn't loiter. Slowly and as noiselessly as a truck
can go I drove away.

That afternoon it rained heavily and I debated whether
to go out again to the bait or to wait until the next morning.
If I had disturbed him because of my oversight, I had better
leave him alone for the day. The slimy, slippery ground would
make driving in gears noisy enough. I would have trouble
approaching the tree. I stayed at camp.

And then it happened.

The usual fires were kept burning and here and there a
lonesome drum throbbed as I went to sleep.

Suddenly, not much, I don't know how much, later, a
weird, short cough, a short, deep-throated cough woke me. It
was the leopard and his call. I grabbed my rifle and bolted
upward, got out of the truck, and stood silent, motionless,
for a long, long while. Another hoarse resonant cough again!
Was it nearer? Did I imagine it only? What shall I do? There
was no use moving. Which way would I go? He may be with
the bait now, or he may be coming here. What is the sense
of going closer to the village? There were no voices, no drums,
and the fires were small mounds of flickering yellow spots
here and there. Again a gruntlike cough. Close this time,
very close, but where in this confounded darkness? No
direction. No help. Then a long, long silence for minutes while
I stood frozen, motionless, naked feet, in shorts, and rifle in
hand with a spotlight attached to the barrel, just waiting,
waiting, waiting.

A sudden, shrill screech and commotion all around. I
bolted and ran toward the first dark stockaded hut and with

the spotlight by now switched on over the rifle barrel I looked and stared in every direction. More bloodcurdling screams and amid the jumping, running black bodies blades of spears reflected light everywhere.

Then my light caught suddenly, unexpectedly, a huge yellow body. I froze, couldn't believe it, but there, not too hurried, with some deliberate leaps, he was dragging something. The cold, glaring light of the electric torch reflecting on the bluish steel shone on his powerful shoulders and neck, the small head, green-flickering, fierce eyes, and I shot, never thinking of the risk of killing man or woman, hitting or missing. I shot again. Down in a heap he crumpled, motionless. Fires were everywhere. Men, women and children, crying, shouting, and running with burning branches, looked like so many silhouettes in this bewitched, frightful night.

There he lay, stone dead. A huge cat, powerful shoulders, tremendous paws, a few trickling drops of blood painting crimson spots over that yellow, golden-yellow, silky skin, and with a small black dog with a broken neck still in his jaws.

Chapter XVI

CHEOKWEES

I STUMBLED on a small Cheokwee settlement near the banks of the Cuchi River. They were in the midst of moving to this particular part of the bush after one of the elders died in the old village. The Cheokwee always leaves a place when the chief or a patriarch dies, and if more than one of the young ones die within a short span. They then select a new place, an excellent means of escaping from an infected, unhealthy area.

It looked as if the entire population came forth to greet me. Their behavior was hospitable. The chief and some of his elders came forward; I gave everyone a handful of cigarettes. They thanked me, striking their chests quickly a few times with hands and saying something sounding to me like *"Cha-tee, cha-tee."* A Cheokwee I had picked up earlier while evidently hunting in the bush started to explain to them something about me. José seemed to have decided the issue of camping sooner than I had, having carefully looked over the handsome and young elements of the "weaker sex." They looked anything but weak. The women were well built, with excellent bearing, and were coiffed in a pony-tail affair, their hair tightly braided across both sides of the skull and tied back with multicolored beads over the nape of the neck. Many wore a blue and white bead band around the head and across the forehead, which gave them an exceedingly pleasing look. Only they had tattoo marks on their faces, but both men and women bore scarification on chest and abdomen, this being a medicinal procedure whenever pain strikes them, or they have "misery in the belly." The little children strapped to their backs looked well and healthy, as did the older ones running freely and standing around in awe. My inclination to be sociable came inevitably to the fore, and so I gave them chocolate and raisins. Some swallowed them and some spat them out, but no one stretched out a hand to receive them. They were shy and undecided.

The men stood in a group eying me. The bows they had in hands were like most I had seen before. They were of smoothened, stiff, and polished hardwood, bent, and the strings on them were either twisted cords of skin or tightly woven, twisted rattan about the thickness of a pencil. Their arrows were more interesting—a bit over two feet in length and about the width of my little finger. The soft iron heads on them had every conceivable shape. Evidently their artistic inclination in blacksmithing showed itself in these. Some oval, some triangular, others like leaves of every imaginable shape, and I even saw one like a corkscrew, but not one looked like any other. I tried to trade with them, but they were either not interested or better traders then I. I approached one—he simply refused. To another I offered salt—he just smiled and acted indifferent. It began to look like a dismal failure. The whole lot, though not antagonistic,

looked as if they just didn't care. I really didn't know how to
proceed.

Then I saw my monkey. I had had one given to me—kind
of a mascot—back in the States. It was a wonderful monkey,
gray, bushy, with a long curved tail. The sight of it inspired
me. It always hung on a rubber cord from the cab ceiling and
bumped up and down—a stuffed monkey, Schwartz's best
in New York. Well, it saved the business transaction. I took
it out and fondled it in my arms. It was about a foot in size
and comical-looking with its brown glass eyes and pink felt
nose. At first they just couldn't understand it. They looked
and looked, and then one started to laugh and right afterward all of them broke into laughter. Each one had to touch
it and examine it carefully. A torrential conversation went
on. I won the game; they liked my monkey; they must like me.

From here on the trading went on delightfully and distinctly in my favor. I played with the monkey and each scene
produced more arrows and knives for me. I could have
cleaned out the entire community!

Thus diplomatic contact was firmly established.

Since it was late, we began to make camp in haste. Soon a
few women approached with eggs and corn-meal mash in
small, beautifully woven baskets and presented them as a
sign of hospitality. They never looked up or into one's eyes.
There was exchange of smiles and garbled words of thanks.

Night fell swiftly, as it always does in Africa; the weird
thumping of drums could be heard. A palaver of some kind
was scheduled for the purpose of discussing me and my
presence there. Undoubtedly they had to decide what to do.

It is wise to be patient and not to push matters. I decided to wait for events to unfold, letting the natives decide whether I would be accepted and how much I would be permitted to see. I settled down to my cooking.

José in the meantime did a powerful amount of ground-work—I suspect not always solely for *my* interest. Judging from the giggling and laughter, I saw that the fair sex was inclined to appreciate this.

A few of them, men and women, from the village walked to my camp and silently waited until I finished cooking, eating, and dishwashing. From mere curiosity they just stood and looked in amazement, entirely oblivious to the possibility that their presence and silent gaze might have annoyed me. I had gotten used to this long before, and perhaps would not have minded even if I had to proceed with more of the elementary and unavoidable physiological functions right in front of them. What can one do?

The drumbeats penetrated all through the bush, echoing and re-echoing, and eerie cries wafted back and forth while women answered in chant.

The stars were out. The brilliant African night, the constellations and the Southern Cross above with the reflected lights of the ground fires here and there made me feel at peace. Small wonder that one who wanders here and is exposed to its mystery and beauty longs to return.

The drums were beating steadily and I told my boy to tell the few waiting near camp that I wanted to go see the dance if they had any that night.

"Yes, we will have a dance, a special dance for the man who came with the Black Magic of the Bees."

What was that? What were they saying, the Black Magic of the Bees?

José grinned and pointed to my Bolex movie camera. Oh yes, now I knew. On the way toward the village this afternoon I had stopped to take some movies of a hunting scene and the Cheokwee I brought along, evidently at the palaver held on my account, described the buzzing noise of the camera motor to the best of his ability as the noise of bees. I was the White Man with the Black Magic of the Bees. If these primitive children of the bush choose to accept me with my camera by connecting it with things in their natural environment, it might mean a chance to film.

I started toward the huts, the *sekulus* following in single file. In the central part near the council hut was a line of men and women facing each other, chanting, but scarcely moving. Flanking each of the lines were drum players. These were not the ordinary type of drum I had seen before, with skin stretched over the hollow and tubular-shaped wood. They were triangular, wedge-shaped wooden pieces, gouged out longitudinally into long, narrow grooves increasing in depth as the dimensions permitted to provide resonance. From its wider end it tapered for a length of three or four feet to its narrower end. It was played on both surfaces with ball-shaped, cloth-covered drumsticks, and often was hit with the elbow depending on how excited the player became. The rhythm and drumming, the motion of the bodies, the glistening muscles and animated faces were blended together. The background was dark, with the reddish glow of fire throwing a weird color upon it, the music like an invitation floated all around, asking from the surrounding huts more and more

people who filed in, staying in clusters. The sharp forms of
the huts lighted by the flames of scattered fires and the
ebony bodies dancing against the sky line produced a
flowing and panoramic silhouette.

They came and led me to one side where a small, square
stool carved out of wood with a stretched ox skin serving
as the seat over it was offered for me to sit on. Only natives
have such rubber joints as to enable them to sit six inches
above the ground on a contraption like this. They do it day
and night. My knees creaked and I wondered how long I
would be able to stand this trial. A fire close by was kept
burning high and dispelled the chill of the night, a welcome
comfort, the elevation here being about five thousand feet.

The dance started.

Women singing and chanting amid the rhythm of the
others' clapping hands upon the undulating tones of the drumming glided forward in a serpentine line toward the opposite row of men. One stepped out and with light, dancing
movements, advanced and retreated, slowly progressing
toward the line of men. Before she could reach or touch anyone, she pointed a finger at one, and then kept dancing
while backing away, teasing, inviting, and calling him to
follow. Now he came forward on the rhythm of the drums,
bending his body and throwing both arms in the air. Reaching the line of women, he pointed at one of them in the row
and she, in turn, came as before toward the line of men. This
went on and on, often two doing the same dancing from one
line to the other, but never more than that. Soon old and
young got into this and at the end not one had been left out
of the dance scene, which continued for hours into the dark-

ness of the night. The drummers changed, but no beat was lost. Young or old, when taking the stick out of one man's hand he was already playing on the drum with the other. Babies slept peacefully, jouncing up and down on the dancers' backs. Time and time again women would take each other's children off the back, carrying them into the standing group to relieve the dancer. And it went on.

How fortunate it is for him that a native can express so much through his music and dance! Sorrow and happiness, birth and death, initiation and marriage—and they will always dance. It is an outlet for human emotions and a perfect way to prevent frustration. I am sure we, too, could function better and require less psychoanalysis in our own society if we would learn to dance with our children on our backs.

With the faint light of the fires and amid the drone of distant drums, flashlight in hand, I headed for the truck, trying to keep to a worn path. The naked feet of the natives had smoothened it to a dusty surface. I lost my way. Again I was more worried about a night-prowling cobra than to watch where I was heading. Among the low growth of bush in complete darkness, save for the beam of the flashlight, for a good long while I wandered and could not find the truck. But here and there I did find couples, separated from the village dancing, underneath the bushes. . . .

It is really remarkable how much a native can fulfill his desires under the effect of music and dances!

In the end I got to my truck. There I looked for José. He was missing. Perhaps I hadn't looked carefully under each bush.

After I made enough noise climbing up and down and in and out of the truck, he showed up from somewhere.

To prepare for a night was a regular ordeal. Much of the duffle, personal gear, some of the food, and the water here, always kept in carafes, had to be loaded into the rear every morning and carried during the daytime on the truck. All this and mosquito nets, the rubber mattress were packed and had to be covered each day with a canvas to prevent seepage of dust into it. My sponge-rubber mattress was a perfect comfort and assured a soft bed, but so saturated with the ever-present fine volcanic dust that one needed a gas mask to sit or lie on it without choking. To clean it in order to sleep on it, every single night as a ritual we attacked it with broken-off branches and small hand brooms. José was in his element again. His military training, more with brooms than rifles, came forth handily. Anyone who has ever come to grips with one of those springy beauty mattresses must have an idea what this meant. To pull and tug an elusive and oversized mass of sponge rubber made by Goodyear to last forever and annoy me for the same length of time was a formidable challenge, and it was so every night. Generally I planned to stop and make camp early to allow time for just such performances and many other chores before sunset. This time I finished brushing everything well enough to dare to climb in and under the canvas-covered rear platform for rolling into a sleeping bag. I was so exhausted I hardly could move. I arranged the lights, tying the kerosene lamps onto the ridge of the canopy. One I had to place in the middle and one on the outer point of the center pole. That was precisely the right place for hitting it every time I went to sleep or got up in the morning. They were placed strategically, indeed, so that after I struck my head on the first and was just struggling to recover, I had to hit the second inevitably after. They did provide light and the very smell of kerosene made it valuable, too, in keeping mosquitoes at a comfortable distance. The flashlight and one of my guns were always lying close beside me. And so all this including myself, was covered with mosquito netting attached from side to side and above to the frame supporting the canvas over me. Imagine wriggling into this maze at night and then extricating yourself in the morning. How much energy, patience, and endurance were required. Occasionally in the middle of the night I was so snarled up that even with the help of a compass I wouldn't find out which way I was lying. So I went to sleep.

My faithful boy, too, by this time, owing to his strenuous effort to establish "friendly relations" all through the evening, was ready to retire. . . . He made his bed under the truck, curling up in a horse blanket, and fell asleep immediately.

The next morning he got things going before I appeared, extricating myself on all fours from the truck and hitting my head, as usual, against those confounded lamps. There was boiled water for shaving and washing; food was cooking. Amid the chatter of many birds I gained momentum. Breakfast was rather elaborate and boosted both my spirit and digestion. After canned butter, bacon, scrambled powdered eggs, with many, many cups of coffee, I was at peace with the world.

So I decided to try to find the chief. With a still camera

in hand I followed the winding path toward the village. When I walked through the narrow entrance between the stockaded walls, no children or women were in sight. With the exception of a few dogs and chickens no one seemed interested in greeting, watching, admiring, or even staring at me. It was strange. I thought perhaps this was the "morning after the night before," in a true native fashion. Yet I caught a glimpse now and then of a child or woman anxiously peering out of a hut and following my movements. Something certainly had occurred to cause this odd reaction. I could not figure it out.

I had to wait and see if this enigmatic situation would resolve itself, so I went back to camp and fussed around awhile. Then my curiosity got the best of me and I went back again. The picture now was changed. Strangely enough, children played around, some watching, some smiling; women carrying baskets or calabashes on their heads moved back and forth. Now practically everyone offered a greeting. This about-face attitude was more perplexing now than before. What could be the reason behind it?

José came and I told him to ask the chief for an explanation. These Cheokwees have a small, carved wooden image of some spirit, possibly representing the ancestral one of this particular clan. It is outside the stockaded area near the entrance path. As a matter of fact, I had noticed the thing the previous night, but paid it no particular heed. It is a foot-high stump left almost in the way of the path and, though it did have primitive carving, I made no inquiry that time about it. It turned out that earlier this morning, as I came along, I passed it on my *right* side instead of on my *left* on the path. This meant to them that I was not paying the spirit due homage and so my entrance into the village would bring them bad luck. They had watched me approach and as soon as I passed this idol on the wrong side, they vanished like camphor. It just happened that later on, on my second attempt to visit them, I passed the stump on the acceptable side and so I became a *persona grata* in the eyes of the spirit and the natives as well.

There you are, or rather, where are you?

How little is needed to find the door closed on their fascinating life and how careful one's approach must be to pry it open to discover the bizarre beliefs existing behind it.

That same afternoon I went to hunt with them. They tracked poorly and when a reedbuck jumped and ran for a good hundred feet almost parallel with their line, six of them shot all kinds of arrows at him, all missing from a distance of about twenty yards. The men were elderly and, though strong-looking and well fed, had not much ambition —not enough for the hunt. I asked why that was. The answer was that the real hunters, the young men, were away.

After leaving them the next day I soon found the answer. I ran into a group of young native Cheokwees singing and walking along on the path in the bush. Each one carried a small bundle tied to his knobkerrie. They were trekking out and heading to report for labor. The mines and large plantations of sisal, coffee, and tea need labor desperately. The head tax here is 120 angolares each year for everyone to pay, and that is about four dollars. It must be paid. How can they get money? What does this mean to them in the bush?

Two years' contract labor with food and blankets given and the head tax paid is the only alternative and certainly a temptation. Deserted villages, broken families, poor hunting, and only the old and very young are left behind. . . .

Chapter XVII

ELEPHANTS

Eᴸᴱᴾᴴᴬᴺᵀˢ were everywhere. So far we had not
happened to see them, but the broken trees and uprooted
bushes all around told clearly that they were somewhere
in the vicinity. The heavily trampled grass and churned-up
small and large clods looked like a deserted circus ground.

López Ferrera peered carefully ahead, bracing himself
against a recently pulled-up euphorbia with a trunk as big
as my waist. Slowly, silently he pushed a large hairy hand
into the pocket of his bush jacket and took out a pinch of
something dry, a powdered mixture. So the crushed tobacco
leaves and dirt, for months never shaken out, served the
purpose adequately. He let the fine dust gently fall from his
fingers and tested the wind. It spiraled downward—hardly
any breeze. This encircling bush was thick indeed, and one
could see no more than a few feet in any direction.

We had been on the march since daybreak and struggled
all morning. The river that curved close here and east of us
was the place all game must come to drink. Fresh droppings,
moist and still steaming, gave the clue that only minutes ago
the elephants had passed here. The path, hewn out with the
trampled grass and bush, zigzagged here and there, and

again straight as an arrow, like a tunnel, led farther and farther. They must be here. But where? Remarkable, I thought, how many times I had hunted and looked for them while they stood almost under my nose, or perhaps more precisely, *I* under their noses, before I could see them. How the gray color of those tremendous bodies can melt into the greenish-yellow shade and sun-splotched bush. How noisy they can be with their rumbling stomachs audible for hundreds of yards, screeching of the young, and toppling trees crashing all around, if they know that they are safe. Yet when they sense danger, how eerie and silent a herd of many dozens can be only a few feet away.

José squinted into the dense bush all around, beads of perspiration forming rivulets on his face. He was worried and visibly afraid. This was not his "dish," nor to his liking. Obviously when I had grabbed him in Nova Lisboa, declaring that from there on he would be my bodyguard and comrade, he bargained for more than he cared to share, and now he knew it. He carried the 30-06 tightly in his nervous hand, but having it failed to dispel the consternation in his eyes.

The air was hot and oppressive—only Ferrera showed no signs of suffering from it. When I asked him to come with me, scrutinizing him at length, I never thought that his big, sloppy, bulging body could stand the trek. He was well recommended as a professional hunter and, besides, there was no other choice. Now he seemed to prove his worth. The country here was just teeming with elephants. I was aware of that beforehand, but in spite of it I had to go through. The upper reaches of the river had been described weeks before to me as the squatting place of an interesting tribe. There, evidently, the natives live entirely devoid of the white man's influence. They are primitive and very wild. If only I could locate them, every effort would be worth while.

And so, after tramping on foot for the past three days, now the goal was near. The previous night, as I camped close to the river's shore, all through the dark hours trumpeting, screeching, and the heavy crashing of trees told the story of bush life and the presence of elephants. And now we were in the midst of this torrid, silent, fearsome bush, constantly and anxiously on guard. I had no wish to kill an elephant. What would I do with it, anyway? I had come here only to find that confounded tribe. But now things looked bad. The wrinkled face of the old Cheokwee elephant hunter, Balombo, became, if it could be, even more wrinkled. The wide nostrils, like two black cobra eyes sprouting upward under the flattened nose on his full-lipped, Negroid face, were fascinating. Like an alert yet silent monkey, he missed not one movement of limb or leaf. With loose joints he bent forward, and then back, testing the air, looking down at the ground, and studying the spoors. His knowledge, his instinct and judgment, based on century-old, inherited nature lore, were amazing and somewhat reassuring.

Slowly he walked forward and, like a shadow, disappeared into the bush ahead. Ferrera looked at me and I, smiling back with no good reason, felt silly. If it was meant to be encouraging, it missed its mark. José perspired more than ever and as he moved anxiously, the whites of his eyes flashed. The .375 Winchester Magnum, loaded with solid bullets this time, was really a needed companion. If our scent is caught, it might be for the best, I mused. Then perhaps they will "beat it." Unless a cow should get nervous about her calf, or a rogue is looking for trouble, they probably would move on, leaving only the huge imprints of those soft-padded feet to show which way they headed. They are masters at moving so quietly and noiselessly that one never knows how close they are.

Footprints like giants', two feet in width and more in length, sinking down one-half foot or deeper, were leading us farther into the bush. The unfathomable López Ferrera bent forward with his bulk, swaying sideways to avoid cracking or breaking branches, followed the Cheokwee. Keeping close to him, I glanced back often to see if José was following. He was there for sure. Where else could he be? No choice, no alternative, yet those apprehensive eyes clearly showed what he thought of all this and especially of me. I could not help it. We were forced to cross the jungle here to reach the shore of the river again. We must find a path to the north. The tribe could not be far. So we kept on.

In an hour, sneaking, climbing, and walking as quietly as one could through the entangled mass, and watching every step, every crack of twigs, always alert and fearful of running headlong into the herd, the river was reached. In a sharp bend it flowed with a slow, majestic, mirrorlike surface, papyrus and palms on its shores. Trampled paths of hippos wandering back and forth crisscrossed the high elephant grass, their fresh droppings splashed right and left.

I stopped to rest, tired and hot, parched and dry, reached for the flask, and drank some wine. José looked despairing; Ferrera, detached. Balombo was in better shape than ever. It was about noon. The vertical rays of the tropical sun mercilessly baked through skin and clothing, giving no chance of escape. This elephant scout was remarkable, tireless, and relentlessly alert to signs and noise.

Slowly, with a deep snort, the ugly snout and two bulbous eyes of a hippo emerged on the surface of the still, smooth water. Its gray-black, wet, glistening skin, like a floating log, blended into the surrounding shadows. Two or three more came up and with deep-throated snorts playfully sprayed water into the air, and then submerged gently. Two yellow-winged butterflies, floating up and down in the air, playing with each other, at times almost on the surface of the water, caught the shafts of golden sunlight filtered through the trees.

We pushed on again.

Balombo, the old wizard, disappeared once more and Ferrera, José, and I waited. He always went a few yards ahead to explore, then signaling with a motion of the hand or an arm, or at times only grimacing, we followed. There were plenty of signs. No doubt somewhere close by the elephants were either feeding or just keeping silent beneath those shady, giant trees. If only we could locate them and know which way to go to avoid them, I certainly would feel relieved!

Balombo came back, with a broad and reassuring smile nodded to us to follow. We went on. All around were mimosa trees forming a patch of forest, many of them pulled out and broken, roots torn as if a hurricane had swept through.

Suddenly he froze and we, like automatons suspended on a wire, stopped. A tuskless giant, twenty feet away, gazed back, reaching with his trunk for a high branch, with tremendous ears flapping back and forth at regular intervals like fans. Ferrera stealthily, almost imperceptibly tested the wind. The crushed tobacco and leaves in a fine powder blew from him toward us. For the time being we were safe. But where are the rest of them? How many? Are they watching us this very moment with those small, beady eyes? Are they trying the air for scent? The trigger guard and stock of the rifle felt hot, and my fingers instinctively dug into it. I don't like that tuskless rogue. That compounded cussedness and savage maliciousness!

We are motionless. Slowly my eyes, becoming used to the surroundings, find the others, his mates, his comrades, cows and calves, in the shadows and everywhere. God only knows how many are here! These gigantic gray bodies with slowly, slightly waving ears, standing bunched together in silence. There a large cow, nearly covered by the sloping branches of a borassus palm, tests the air with her trunk slowly, deliberately, moving around and keeping this young calf of hers, a very small one, between her legs. The breeze is faint. Balombo picks up a handful of grass seeds to test the air. They fall straight to the ground. He looks back at me and winks and I, taut with anticipation, wink back automatically, but not knowing why. Does this mean a signal? What's the purpose? I wonder. There is no retreating here. Elephants are all around and we are smack in their midst.

Ferrera pushes back the safety catch on his heavy, double-barreled rifle and keeps his gaze stolidly forward. I, with one eye on this suspicious cow and the other on the bolt of my rifle, checking it, now feel this solid heat more than ever.

Something happened.

A twig or fallen branch snapped loudly and rang through the broken silence. The cow whipped her outstretched and rigid trunk upward into the air, suddenly whirled around. Her calf, panic-stricken, screamed. Then came terrorizing, high-pitched trumpeting, and pandemonium broke loose. Shapeless, running, thundering bodies were everywhere, crashing trees in their wake. The earth rocked. Trees and sky were blotted out. Nothing was visible but a monstrous gray mass with spreading, rigid ears like enormous rudders on a plane, and a trunk thrust forward and upward in front of me. It was massive, high, and all-space-filling. I stood underneath like an ant.

With white tusks flashing he came screaming, trumpeting, roaring.

José cried out and I saw him turn in terror, running first back, and then abruptly changing, going off to one side. He fell. The maddened, raging bull was reaching out with trunk like a whip to pound and smash upon him.

I fired, how I don't know.

He staggered and slowly, as if hesitating, collapsed against a half-ripped-out tree, pulling it down and crashing close to where José was still clambering among roots and fallen branches. Two other shots rang out in short succession, deafening, close to my ears. Ferrera was kneeling and shooting again.

In this unaccountable panic the entire herd was off on a terrible stampede of fear and fury. The forest came alive. It seemed as if every tree suddenly turned into another elephant. Everything swayed, moved, and crashed around us. What was happening? Who was here? Was anybody hurt?

Balombo was on the top of a tree and José at the bottom of one. Before I had time to realize what happened, the herd was gone.

There lay two bulls, one close, very close to my boy, paralyzed with fear and cowering under a fallen tree like a rabbit, not daring to move, the other, about fifteen yards down-wind, his colossal body still quivering, but dead. The acrid smell of cordite, the fallen giants, and our two black companions sheepishly extricating themselves from under branches and roots were a perfect anticlimax.

I was mad, boiling mad. José's pride was badly hurt. Balombo was satisfied, and Ferrera, stolid, unperturbed, remarking simply in broken English, "Senhor, the weather is dry in Angola, very dry, and at times hot."

To Balombo this was nothing but a usual encounter with fate, and he acted accordingly. He took his knife, cut a piece off of the nearest fallen bull's tail for "good luck," and sat down on a stump in pleasant anticipation of the coming meal.

López Enrico Antonio y Ferrera, my enigmatic friend and white guide, was not pleased at all. He had shot the tuskless bull and there wasn't any ivory to sell. It had charged him while I got involved in an argument with mine over who was going to have José. And the ivory on my bull was light and not worth much. Poor luck for all concerned.

We sat down to talk matters over and that helped to steady shaking knees. It was early afternoon. From here on surely nothing would hinder us in reaching the tribe and pitching camp before sunset. It looked as if there would be no need to do that, for in a short time strange, small-statured, and wild-looking men came from the bush, about a dozen of them, armed with long, straight, heavy-shafted spears. They stood silently a distance from us, watching and sizing up the meat they were so hungry for. They were the ones I hoped to find. The stampeding herd and the shooting were too much to miss. They came and so we met.

Before long the entire band was there, women, children, and men. Balombo tried to be the contact man, but I could see that the conversation was halting and rather one-sided. They did not understand him or his dialect, and they trusted us less. Yet the meat was much too appealing to overlook and after we cut out the tusks, they started. It was a veritable carnage.

All afternoon and evening, and late into the night by the light of large fires, off the carcasses meat was eaten, devoured, chewed, and gulped down. With wildly slicing knives in every direction, like ants on a corpse, they were moving. Bloody guts glistening on the ground in trails like giant serpents were everywhere. This band looked like a cross between Cheokwees and Bushmen. A paradoxical mixture of savagery and timidity, very primitive they were indeed. A narrow leather apron covered the front and rear of the women, and only a very small part of it. Children were entirely naked.

They gorged to the point that many hardly could move and then, like vultures after feasting on carcass and unable to fly off, some just lay down and belched until there was more space in their distended stomachs to gulp more meat again. It was beyond imagination how anyone, young or old, could stuff so much meat into his gizzard!

A dance was held for a double purpose: to celebrate and to be able to eat more afterward. All the men, and only they, participated, holding to each other in a row. They placed arms on the shoulders of the one in front, danced and walked like elephants, and acted with their arms as tusks, tumbling forward to re-enact the hunting scene.

All through the night children and women carried the meat back somewhere in the bush and came back for more. Morning came and only the huge skeletons with their enormous bones remained to tell the tale.

Chapter XVIII

THE QUIPUNGO FUNERAL

Among some tribes funerals are still conducted more or less in the brutal manner of their primitive ancestors. On the other hand, many aspects have been changed by now and the basic elements are no longer practiced and so are lost to observation; for instance, tying the corpse round and round with twines and ropes made from tree bark, wrapped like a mummy in a half-sitting position, and keeping it on a high, elevated platform for many days and weeks. Sitting with the dead husband, rubbing and massaging the body to press out the fluids, and then letting it shrink and dry out under the sun's heat in order to keep it in that state for months afterward without burying it. Things of this kind have slipped into the irretrievable past. Human sacrifice at funerals was still practiced in the nineteenth century among some of the very primitive tribes in the lower Congo and along the eastern fringes of Angola, but is by now only history.

Christian teaching, government regulations, enforcing of hygienic principles, rules of interment have altered those rituals. Then, too, the natives, often without coercion, gave up what their forefathers practiced in hope that by doing so they gain easier entrance into their idea of heaven.

North of Sá da Bandeira and a few kilometers south of Quipungo I met several strangely decorated women. They were walking in groups of two or three. White shells, some painted with a pinkish hue, round in shape, a few inches in diameter, strung in a vertical line of three or four, hung loosely on their backs directly over the spine. Tall and thin they were, the upper bodies covered with black or chocolate-brown shawls draped across one shoulder in a Roman-toga fashion. Here and there, trudging along without any sign of fatigue, a few carried young and older children on their backs. We caught up with them and stopped. José, with a broad smile and with cigarettes in hand, immediately tackled a few of the old and wiser ones. But the young girls, with or without children on their backs, either sensing or knowing too well that their magnetic charm often led to dire con-sequences, ran, leaped, and took to the bush. Babies were bouncing, short skirts were flying.

The cigarettes worked, however; the old stood their ground. In a short time it was found out that an important chief had died a few days ago. His funeral rites had been in progress and would continue a few more days before the burial. That was something to know.

We promptly piled into the truck again and raced as fast as the washboard road allowed to the *administrador* at Quipungo. It was noon as I pulled in. He was not home, but his assistant told me that the Ngambwe tribe had a par-amount chief nearby in the bush in their large village about fifteen kilometers away. For many miles he reigned and was looked up to by his people with veneration. He was old, very old indeed, and steeped to the bone in the rites of his forefathers. His people adhered strictly to his dicta.

If any, *this* funeral rite would conform to the ancestral format.

I felt it essential to prearrange an approach and map out a plan to avoid the possibility of arousing suspicion or bruising the sensitivity of such an important man, whose consent was so vital to my presence at these "last rites." From among half a dozen native police boys standing around the courtyard, always just looking with open mouth and wide-open eyes, totally baffled by the white man's ways, conferences, talks, and planning, I picked one out. He came from the same village and was a natural selection. I commissioned him to go ahead with some salt and cloth. He was drilled at length and told specifically not to spare the glowing terms (many of those natives are born masters of description), and that he must draw an unusual and, to their imagination, an interesting picture of me. What is interesting from a native viewpoint about a white man is conjectural. So after looking me over carefully and sizing up my trucks, friends, and the different knickknacks I let him decide what "line" to give the chief about me. He left. In the early afternoon we, too, started out to find the palace and its retinue. This road, many years old, was wide and bumpy. The zigzagging path and the spoors of the cattle showed the marks of natives traveling on it for countless long years.

In an hour or so we came upon his lodgings. Obviously the king's domain was well organized and wealthy. The palace was partly in the bush, but surrounded by grassland.

It was an ideal grazing country for cattle. My envoy, the sepaio, was already waiting for us and far outside in the open we were received by two tall, dignified members of the court. From afar drums and monotonous crying and wailing could be heard. There were greetings by clapping hands and slightly bowed heads and exchange of well-wishing. It turned out that my appearance in person following whatever picture my delegate painted did the trick. We were expected and invited inside the stockade.

Stepping over the one-foot-high row of sticks lying parallel to the ground in the entranceway, a narrow, tunnel-like stockaded area led sharply into a funnel-shaped place. Along the path a row of debarked trees about six to eight feet in height stockaded both sides. It wound around separate and circular areas evidently reserved for the cattle and some for the young heifers. Beyond these, narrow entrances led into sections where corn and the usual contents of granaries were stored. We walked through another narrow stockaded entrance and turned a corner sharply. I found myself suddenly in an open space and before a large hut built from vertically and adjacently placed logs. Its conical-shaped roof was covered with grass. All around strewn on the ground were many gourds, finely woven baskets. A T-shaped heavy plank held several skulls of small gazelles and horns of oxen.

I was standing in the king's reception place.

In front of this hut on a small stool he sat. In his hand he held and occasionally puffed on a long-stemmed pipe decorated elaborately with metal. The face was kind, interestingly sculptured, with a thinnish little gray beard on the chin. He looked to be old, very old. I never can estimate the age of a patriarch among the natives. Around him were women, young and old, and grown-up sons, and toddlers here and there. It gave credence to the stories about the "vigor and vim" those men retain to a ripe old age. The oldest in his harem, undoubtedly his first wife, weather-beaten, with a determined, wise mien, all-observing, missed nothing and seemed to command the whole situation. The only person sitting was the king. His court, children, wives and others stood in attendance.

There he was, a tall and lanky, dignified, jet-black human, sitting placidly with outstretched feet, his big toes protruding and quiescent, and sizing me up shrewdly while smoking his pipe. José tugged on my bush jacket frantically, trying to explain that we must watch his big toe. This is a crucial sign, and an age-old custom. It indicates whether or not we win royal favor, or whether it is time to give up and leave. If it waves up and down, beware!

In bygone days a very large and appropriate gift could change the inclination of the big toe and cause it to become stationary, after which the visitor could be likewise so. How fortunate that native kings of yore were never afflicted with gout.

In my case the salt and other presents seemed to have worked sufficiently and I was received with an immobile big toe.

It was interesting to see how this dignified old man kept the large population, the village, and his own court in awe. He offered me palm wine. I lifted the gourd, anxious not to offend him, concealing my lips behind my thumbs, and swallowed big, rolling my eyes accordingly, but not touching the gourd with my mouth. I was a bit concerned of consequences if detected, but everything proceeded satisfactorily and the gourd was passed from man to man. Here I was in the midst of some exciting ceremonies. Not only had someone accommodated me by conveniently dying at a time that coincided with my presence there, but on top of it the deceased happened to be a subchief, which called for extraordinary preparations to facilitate his journey to "Spirit Village."

After I obtained his approval to witness the entire ritual, as a parting gesture he took his pipe out of his mouth and shook hands with me. Then deliberately he opened a tiny, square wooden box hanging attached to his belt, took out a small amount of snufflike brownish powder, and rubbed it between the palms of his hands. I worried. What would I do if, as a sign of his friendship, I was offered some of this powder? Certainly I could not deceive him by feigning the snuffing as I had the wine drinking. No, curiosity should not deserve such penalty. Happily the matter took its own course. This was too good to share with me. He took a powerful sniff of it, with a resultant exploding sneeze. Why he didn't blow away several of his children and surely his grandchildren in a cloud of dust I don't know. I was later told that court etiquette demands on such occasion that all present respond loudly with the word *Sazuka!* in unison. *Prosit,* if you like. "Come back quickly!" It means that the spirit of the man sneezing is apt to allow itself to be blown away. Woe to the unfortunate. What would he do after such calamity? It would be like Pinocchio without conscience.

No, no, no! *"Sazuka!"* again, and so it is urged to stay inside of him.

I retired graciously and left His Majesty with his snuffbox, pipe, wives, children, and big toes behind.

I set up my camp and next morning returned and hurried directly to the village to select the scenes I wanted to film. I learned much about the significance and the action within rigid rules of some personages connected with the funeral. When an important man like a chief or a subchief dies, here it is told about in a song.

The name of the deceased is never mentioned.

An old musician or delegate is elected to go to the paramount chief and inform him by way of a song about the death. He plays on a marimba a repetitious theme sounding something like this: *"Tcha-tee-kah . . . Tcha-tee-kah."* This musical instrument is composed of half gourds tied together, serving as a sounding board. Above the opening of each gourd is a flat, square, light, and resonant piece of wood strung in a half-moon shape so that the instrument is about three to four feet in length and one-half foot in width. Strings or twines are fastened to each end. The player can carry it around his neck. When he plays on it, either sitting or kneeling, he keeps it between his knees and strikes it with light wooden sticks.

Drums were played all through the day. Women and men trickled in, squatted down, and just waited. The village was large and I wandered back and forth for a long while before I found the coffin. It was placed close to the exit from the stockaded section leading out into the fields opposite the main entrance gate and far away from his own hut.

Whether or not this was incidental or in compliance with orders of the ritual I didn't know. The coffin, a crudely nailed-together box, was completely covered with black cloth. And—behold—marked with the sign of a cross! The nearby Catholic mission apparently had its influence on them. It rested on a slightly elevated platform and above it was a roof built from fresh branches with leaves left on to prevent the sun from penetrating through. The entire flimsy construction looked like a shelter without walls, like a grotesque four-poster bed with log canopy above. Close beside it grass mats were laid down where men sat chanting, and a bit farther away in a separate group three women were squatting. These were the dead-watchers who night and day sat around and followed the coffin every time it was carried through the village, hired specifically to wail and cry periodically.

I wandered aimlessly with Bolex in hand, José following me like my shadow. Watching many happily smiling, joking, laughing faces all around, I was convinced that this was not only a sad affair but a celebration as well. Not far from where the coffin was placed and close to the exit there was a corral. A few men walked into it and with slow deliberation proceeded to put grease or fat from a chunk of tallow on their spear blades. It meant killing. Three oxen were selected. Carrying the light spears in hand, men entered the corral hedged around with thornbushes. Not too bravely and keeping themselves a considerable distance from the beast wildly running, each one threw his spear with one lightning stroke directly into a selected ox. It was over in a few minutes. The head was severed and immediately placed on an elevated platform in front of the palaver house. In a short time the meat was prepared and divided among the many.

This was a celebration for the "spirit" of the deceased and, therefore, had to be a *royal* affair. Untold efforts are expended to produce a grand funeral to insure a better reception of him in "Spirit Land."

Sons are the ones who bury the father and the daughters weep over him. More daughters can cry more effectively. More sons can arrange the burial more elaborately.

Much wealth must be spent, to hire women for chanting and crying day and night, to entertain lamenting and laughing men, friends, and relatives, and even friends of the relatives' friends, all recalling and extolling the virtues of the deceased. Shooting the blunderbusses and beating the logs went on and on. The primitive does not accept natural causes for death; it is always the machinations of a bad-spirit fetish which causes a departure from life. A fetish must be mixed with, or possessed by, the bullet, knife, lion, or stomach-ache. In the past, when they were pagans or atheists, they had little fear of death.

The women who entered the village, coming from far and near outlying areas, first went straight to the hut of the mourning family. There they expressed sorrow and sympathy by merely sitting and crying with the rest of them. Visitors soon were seen to emerge, stooping low through the entrance. Then they selected an open, sunlit spot, squatted down, and waited patiently.

Children were everywhere, the little ones decorated exactly as their mothers, their hair and little shells down their backs arranged precisely the same. Brass, copper, and plain wire bracelets gleamed on arms and legs. Some belles had as many as twenty coils made into a necklace, keeping their chins raised high and necks so stiff they could scarcely move.

And now a hushed atmosphere descended over all. Here and there crying broke the stillness and sobbing faces peered out of huts. The family of the deceased was staying in one hut from which shrill cries echoed together with the intermittent wails of the onlookers assembled for the occasion. Then suddenly I became conscious of a peculiar noise and chanting. I looked around and there I saw twelve men squatting tightly around a long, heavy, and slightly curved log. A monotonous dirge filled the air from the beating of the hollow-sounding log with stubby sticks. Two standing with oval-shaped drums between their legs were drumming. In the midst of this three strange characters appeared. All sorcerers; one with a rigidly frozen smile, hollow-eyed, old, a very old man, the very incarnation of mysticism. He slowly started a swaying dance. The other, tall, thin, and wiry-looking, with a deep scar over his left eye, kept constantly shaking his divining rattle. Holding a knobkerrie with its weighty, bulbous top in the other hand, he stepped in to dance. The third, with a much younger, stark-naked body glistening under the merciless hot sun, leaped like a frog among the other two. A few feet away was the coffin under its log roof like a stolid memento of bygone life.

All of a sudden everything stopped. A strange, eerie anticipation was in the heavy air. Six men rose, walked to the coffin, lifted it carefully on shoulders, and carried it slowly into the open. The three wailing women, the dead-watchers, followed and with shrill cries flagged a black cloth every so often as the procession formed. I breathlessly filmed, working from all angles to get this sad scene. The moaning and crying were the only sounds and from the direction of the relatives' hut came a lonesome drumbeat off and on. The coffin was carried slowly and at times with difficulty by those old natives. It slipped, swayed, and often looked as though it might fall. The men were small and tall, some weak and aged, others strong; their gait was uneven and uncertain. They stopped in front of each hut. Then one called out loudly for the "spirit" to point out who caused this man's death. After a short exclamation another took over the heavy knobkerrie and, wildly gesticulating with it, continued orating in front of the next hut in line. With the exception of the three dead-watchers no women were part of this impressive scene. They sat or squatted in groups with anguished faces silently watching. The air was hushed, sultry, and heavy. No noise, no interference, no laughter was audible now. After making the rounds from hut to hut the coffin was carried back and placed again under the shelter.

In the center of the village now men and women joined in a wild dance while the constant drumming whipped them into a hysterical mass of humanity. Diviners jumped into the center and danced, emulating a warrior, a bird, or an animal. This was the only time and place I ever saw a sorceress dancing; she, with a large black raven's feather in her bushy, short-cropped, kinky black hair, gyrated in circles. This wrinkled-up old woman spiraled again and again into a narrow center all by herself, with bent body and staring eyes, and with rattles in both hands. Six men in opposite lines began a war dance, whirling and circling each other with spear in hand. Jumping and swiftly running, thrusting spears and knives. They missed one another by inches. It was like a three-ring circus with different scenes going in each.

As the day went on three more times the coffin was carried along the same route and halted again in front of each hut. Certainly ample opportunity was given for this "noble spirit" to bid adieu to everyone in each hut and thereby to insure its *permanent* departure. The owner of one hut, just to assure himself that the spirit of the dead would have nothing against his generous participation in this ceremony, after having himself sufficiently fortified and saturated with palm wine, shot off his blunderbuss in a farewell blast with a tremendous roar, to the delight of all bystanders, almost jarring the camera out of my shaking hands.

An omnifarious celebration of this sort is difficult to understand. Its symbolism defies exemplification. Yet its purpose for the native is simple. The spirit is furnished a satisfactory send-off so that it is happy and willing to leave the village. After such pleasant celebration it should bear no grudge against the folks, nor get recalcitrant and so choose to stay behind.

The burial took place at sunset.

In the late afternoon as the sun made long, angular shadows and tinted everything with its reddish hue, the relatives came out of the hut and sat down on the ground in a group. Young and old alike looked grief-stricken. The tears rolled down their black and brown velvety or crinkled skins. They comforted each other, sometimes one holding a hand over another's bitterly sobbing mouth. Bodies shook in visible sorrow. I would have never imagined that they allowed themselves to go to such length as to show their grief outwardly. While the drums beat, the crowd stood looking impassively at the group of crying women. This time the coffin was removed in finality and carried directly outside the stockaded area never to be taken back among the mourners again. The pall of hushed silence was broken only by the rattles of the sorcerers providing a farewell incantation. The wailing grew fainter while the bowed backs of the coffin bearers with their black burden disappeared from sight.

What a strange and incongruous spectacle! How can the sorrow and grief, the long, almost circuslike celebration, the dancing, chanting and laughter, eating and drinking, and the theatricals of the hired wailing women combine with the coffin and the cross on it? If the burial lacks sufficient pomp and ceremony to satisfy the spirit, it might get troublesome and decide to hover around much longer. It might even go rampant and sneak into an innocent, unknowing bystander, into a relative or friend, and do all kinds of tricks. Calamity, illness, or death might follow. The possibility that the "spirit" of the deceased may act irresponsibly and may wander all around recklessly and unruly is a constant fear. Therefore, they will go to any length to convince it to go straight and without hesitation to the "Spirit Village," where it belongs and so must live happily thereafter. That is the reason behind all this dancing, eating, shooting the blunderbuss, crying, laughing, wailing, and drumming.

Since the other spirits are occupied during the day, the burial always takes place at sunset. All well-behaved spirits are working in the forest or in the fields; if they are women, they carry water in calabashes on their "spirit heads" just like the living do. They return to "Spirit Village" at sunset. So the new spirit must arrive at that time in order to be received by them all.

What does all this mean to the native? The symbol of Christian religion, the cross on the coffin and on the little string around the neck here, as I saw it, was accepted from the white man only for physical comfort's sake and certainly not for the spiritual.

Here is on one side: white man's religion, Christianity, the cross on the coffin, and on the opposite: spirit invoking, the savage log beating, and the dances of the sorcerers. How does all this fit into the native mind? Is he confused? Is he helped? Does he need the comfort, does he need the reassurance of the Christian philosophy? The symbol of the cross on the crude coffin and the pagan rites displayed around show how much he is, himself, at the crossroad. The tears flowing and the grief-stricken, almost convulsive faces of women and men lamenting the inevitable fate of all living beings indicate only one thing: the impact of human tragedy here in the bush is as intense as anywhere in the world over. They need comfort and assurance, some form of a philosophy, as we all do. What do they do? They accept both almost as if they consciously recognize that holding—at least for the time being—onto the pagan rites while learning more about ours gives them double security.

At their burial place near a path each mound was left with a few broken bottles or gourds as crockery for the spirit of the deceased. A stick above the grave for a man and a basket for a woman, but nowhere was the cross.

Chapter XIX

THE USUAL AND THE UNUSUAL

THE SHIMMERING HEAT filled the day, and mirage, displaying sparkling lakes, fantastic groups of animals, lovely shady parklands and refreshing oases, taunted us for hours. We were tired and hungry. Meat was needed and the base camp was many kilometers away. I had stalked and wandered considerably farther than I had intended, following a large herd of elephants, trying to catch up with them. It was no use. They were faster than I and constantly on the go. I fell behind. José, my recently declared, pompous gunbearer, lost equal amounts of water and enthusiasm by perspiring and by wilting. He, too, was on the edge of exhaustion. I gave up for the day.

And so we were heading back to base camp when I ran into a bunch of Cape buffalo. Out of the herd of at least a hundred heads, many cows and many more calves, it was difficult to select the right-size bull. One magnificent old fellow was standing a bit removed from the rather disturbed and anxiously watching herd. Stock-still, head erect, and ready to charge, he followed every move of mine. I stalked, using as cover a large anthill between us and was able to get within seventy yards of him. It took time. Crawling on hands and knees cautiously and looking into his mud-caked, tremendous black face, knowing that he was just about making up his mind when to attack, I felt every heartbeat pounding all through my body. I got to a place from where I dared not go farther. Carefully lying prone and holding the .375 Magnum, I had to shoot five times to drop him as he was coming like a runaway Mack truck after the first hit. He careened, stopped, and was hit again, bellowed, came on, and was hit again, but about fifteen yards away from me decided to give up, and lay down. The herd stampeded while the shooting went on and, to the satisfaction of both of us, took the opposite direction to disappear.

Because of the late hour I decided to leave the carcass lying there for the night, although the meat (about 1000 pounds) was needed to feed many native boys. I took the cape and horns to camp, hoping that the hyenas would leave the rest of it alone until morning. I knew it only too well: they can devour any sort and any amount of meat, even if it is spiced with rusty nails, but I had no other choice. After an all-night concert by hysterical laughing hyenas (seldom having much to laugh about) and roaring lions, both baritones and bassos, I expected by early morning to find a concentration of noble and uninvited guests around.

At daybreak, with José carrying my guns, I stalked to the carcass, being on the look-out for leopards, lions, or other unwanted adversaries. The light was too weak for filming, so unfortunately the action that followed during the next twenty minutes I could only watch. It was one of the most unique animal plays I have ever seen and perhaps will ever be privileged to see. Around the carcass in a semi-circle sat a gallery of vultures, many of them on nearby trees and others hungrily waiting on the ground among dignified-looking and stiff-walking marabou storks. Moving among them like so many ushers were a half dozen or so spotted hyenas, with a few jackals holding the best "box seats." The principal actors, center stage, were three full-grown male lions lashing out with tails silently and with tongues very audibly. The raucous screeching of the vultures with a high-pitched barking of jackals and the weird hair-raising screams of the hyenas blended into a symphony like Saint-Saëns's "Danse Macabre" and the acting was to everybody's greatest pleasure.

The lions were spinning around, running back and forth, leaping here and there while trying to keep birds and hyenas away, but were beginning to tire after their all-night performance. Then slowly from the mist rising close to the ground two bachelor friends of the shot buff arrived. They just stood for a while as if sizing up what was going on here. Then one lowered his head, pawed the ground, and with saliva drooling and eyes bulging started to attack. The thundering hoofs of those one-ton "black express trains" running after three lions was something to hear! Because of the mathematical inequalities (three never being divided evenly by two) their direction and act was switched and switched again and again in split seconds. Sometimes one lion was chased, sometimes another, but most of the time all three were chased in all directions.

A buffalo is a most determined and persistent beast to

give chase when he wants to. These two felt, seeing their comrade lying there and the lions around him, that they had good reason to blame them for the death of their comrade. But the big, tawny cats were obviously hurt and visibly upset by the injustice. They felt out of sorts. So the little scene of "all around the mulberry bush" (and this time it was the thornbush) went on merrily until, quick as lightning, one wise old buffalo cut ahead of one lion and met him head-on, to the great surprise of the King of Beasts! The only thing he could do was to leap, and up he went to the top of a 25-foot thorn tree. Thorns about an inch in length and hundreds of them made no difference. Mind over matter is what counts. There he was in the tree like a cat chased by a dog, with a raging black cussedness below, bloodshot-eyed and drooling. The buff made up his mind to stay, and so did the lion—but on different levels. I watched the time and actually for twenty minutes the scene did not change. Every so often he pawed, went like a ramrod against the trunk of the tree. That in turn swayed back and forth and the lion on it held on with his claws for dear life. Then he bellowed, a deep, resonant, savage roar. The other old, grumbling bachelor friend came up and stood close to the same tree. They stood, looked around and upward, kept standing for minutes, and one could hear panting. The air filled with expectation—birds, animals watching in a fearful silence. Then approvingly and slowly, hesitantly, they decided to leave the scene of their fallen comrade. They stopped again and again to look back and finally disappeared among the bush.

After a while the other two lions ambled out from the

bush slowly, heading toward the carcass again, evidently convinced that the "express trains" had left for good. The third sheepishly—to the gloating satisfaction of the audience of vultures, hyenas, and jackals—sneaked down from the tree to join them. This time he was not only very, very careful to assure himself that the buffs had left, stepping gingerly in case another round should come, but stopped and sized up each tree—looking them over thoroughly so as to decide which one to jump into should the chase start again.

An amazing act and perfect indication of the intelligent thought processes of wild game.

I needed that meat too. Meat-hungry natives were with me and all around in the bush. The carcass was a fine gift to present to a nearby village and to its chief. So I watched and stayed, hoping that I, too, would get my share.

As the sun climbed higher and the heat became more and more intolerable, the lions retreated, but the birds stayed. So I dispatched one boy to ask the chief to come; I knew that if I left the carcass in a couple of hours there would be little meat on it. What the vultures had not finished the hyenas would surely take care of. I selected a sizable thorn tree and settled down in its shade, comfortable out of the scorching sunlight, and waited.

In an hour or so the chief arrived. A motley crowd, women, children, old, and young, followed him. I offered part of the meat to him amid ceremonial exchange of greetings. We were both impressed with each other's capabilities. Soon they were crawling like so many ants, in and over and out of the buffalo carcass. Chunks of meat were flying, *pangas* were viciously and most carelessly swung in all directions, and why fingers and hands were not chopped off along with the meat I shall never know.

As I sat under the tree watching and absorbed in the atavistic scene, I completely forgot to film all this savage action. Early in the morning, owing to poor light conditions, I came up here without a camera, and later on, when I decided to stay guarding the carcass, I never thought to send a boy back to get one. So here I was to witness an unusual, wild orgy of those meat-starved primitives, and no camera on hand.

José and the chief were in an earnest conversation. Their grimaces, their spirited gesticulations and voices pitched high and low were evidently directed at me. I was unconcerned. This African sun took all energy and desire out of me. I just wilted in the heat.

More talk, finger pointing, and wide, all-encircling motion of arms seemingly for nothing. José came to me. Haltingly, hesitantly he started to explain that we were invited for a grand celebration tonight. I was to be the guest of honor. I, "the hunter" who killed the vicious buffalo and gave the meat to them, should get a royal reception.

"Okay, José, we shall go. Nothing suits me better than to have fun, especially in the evening when the sun is down and this confounded heat subsides. I want to see how these meat-crazy people can act when they are drink-crazy. Tell him, José, we will be happy to be there."

More talk followed, more hesitation, more gesticulation, and then silence. My boy kept looking toward me. The chief surveyed me from head to toe while a couple of old women holding blood-dripping strips of meat ignored the butchery to cast scrutinizing looks at me.

What is this all about?

I nodded to José again and waited. Then he came to me a bit slower and definitely very reticent.

"What is it now, José?"

"Senhor, you will be the guest of the chief."

"All right, I know I will be the guest of the chief."

"You are expected to stay in the front of his palaver house."

"All right, I will do so."

"You will sit on the little stool only honored people are allowed to sit on."

"Nothing will delight me more."

"The chief is a very rich man. He has many huts, not many cattle, he is sorry to say, but he has fruits, he has beer to drink, and, senhor, all that the chief has is going to be yours for the night."

"Fine, my boy. Tell him I am not too thirsty and certainly not too hungry, but I shall be there. I shall be there at sunset and I will sit on his stool and enjoy the celebration."

José paused again. The message he bore seemed stuck in his throat. He continued circuitously:

"But, senhor, the chief is very rich."

"Good, José. I am glad he's rich."

"But, senhor, the chief has seven wives!"

"More power to him!"

"Senhor, you are the guest of the chief tonight and he offers all his possessions for your enjoyment. His stool, his beer, his huts, and his seven wives."

"No, no, no! I will sit on his stool, drink his beer, eat his food, but no, not the seven wives! I don't need them. Just go tell him that I appreciate all this and let's forget about the seven wives."

More waiting, more hesitation, more shifting back and forth.

"No, senhor, that cannot be done. The chief is very important. I tried to tell him that maybe my boss, this white senhor, would feel equally honored without the seven wives. But you see, the chief cannot lose face. His people feel that anything the chief has is the best and the chief's guest must have the best. He tells me, senhor, he cannot lose face!"

"All right, José, tell him . . . tell him that I don't doubt he has the best, but I am not thirsty, I am not hungry, and I don't want to sleep with seven wives."

José went back to the chief. By now the elders were around him in a group, men and women all talking simultaneously, all talking excitedly. I did not realize fully the seriousness of the matter. The chief himself looked really embarrassed, talked little, but much more so did his retinue, and José was very much perplexed.

I felt I must do something. I intended to stay here at least a week or more. I needed this man's help and through him the good will of the whole tribe. What should I do? At the outset the matter looked funny, but now it had taken a different aspect. These simple and primitive human beings live with a code of their own. Nothing hurts them more and nothing causes more loss of dignity and respect than to be laughable. This situation was surely heading toward it.

Then an idea came to me.

Oh, José, my boy, my faithful companion, my guardian angel with a tender heart and considerate solicitude! This is the time I shall get even with you! I'll never forget what you did for me in the hotel at Sá da Bandeira. One good deed deserves another, and the time for it is here.

"Come over here. I want to tell you something. And ask the chief to come along."

They both came and stood in front of me.

"Now listen here, I want you to tell word by word and sentence by sentence to this important chief, this exalted personality, the bravest warrior of all these brave people here: I accept his generous offer."

José with a big broad smile in a short sentence said just that. Everybody was relieved and everyone was beaming.

"Now, José, keep on with the rest of it. Aren't you my gunbearer, José?"

"*Sim, senhor.*"

"All right. Tell him so. Aren't you carrying my guns, the heavy and the light ones, since I promoted you to this honorable position?"

"*Sim, senhor.*"

"Then tell that to them."

"Yesterday when I stalked this buffalo, weren't you standing close behind me and holding that gun right there, the one now resting against the tree, and didn't you give it to me to kill this buffalo?"

"*Sim, senhor, sim, senhor.*"

"Fine, José. Just tell this to the chief, too."

They all listened; they all seemed to understand; and they all tensely waited for more.

"Now tell the chief that I could never shoot this buffalo if you, the brave, trusty, faithful boy and gunbearer of mine, had not carried this gun and then given it to me. I could never have killed the buffalo and certainly never have given the meat to them for this celebration if not for you, José. Can you see this, José?"

"*Sim, senhor.*"

"Then go tell the chief that *you* are the one who shall sleep with the seven wives . . . Now don't hesitate, go on and tell him so!"

A wide grin on José's face, a halting explanation, a bashful, hesitant expectation . . . exploding laughter and a tremendous roar of hand clapping, shrieking, singing, and jumping proved that I had found the right solution.

We all went to the village that night. I sat on the stool in front of the chief's house. I drank his beer. I ate some of the meat. I listened to the drums and saw the dances.

So did José.

In the morning, as we started out on a long trek heading back to civilization, I looked for my gun-carrying boy, José. He was there, but without the guns. Even the lightest one was too heavy for him to carry!

And so we reached Nova Lisboa.

At the end of my safari, comprising the months of ordeals, occasional adversity, countless sleepless nights, and all the fascinating experiences, the time came for us to say good-by to each other. Soon I had to take the train for Lobito and then board a ship for home.

Before leaving I wanted to get José another job. I found a good place for him with a married geologist whose family, wife and children, had just arrived from the States and was establishing a household and needed a houseboy. I certainly could not recommend anyone better than my José.

The next day with the help of a translator I explained to him that I had found employment for him where he would be well taken care of, well paid, and free of worry. He was thankful and visibly touched by it, but when it reached the point of my telling him that he would be paid three hundred fifty angolares a month (and that is a little less than twelve dollars), he very meekly yet positively insisted that he could not accept the job because he needed more pay. He stated that he had a wife and several children to take care of and he could work for the railroad and get more money. The solution was not simply to pay him more. All the other houseboys were getting about the same amount from the other geologist families and we could not create a situation by having this fellow receive more. After much discussion it was decided to tell him that his pay rate as houseboy must remain fixed, but he could supplement it by doing various added chores such as cleaning the laboratory floor.

That was perfectly all right with Sunday Joe.

That afternoon, returning to my quarters with him beside me in the truck, I told him that my expedition had come to an end, paid him for his faithful service and for sticking out many months' tribulations with me, and reminded him again that next morning he would have to start his new job. While holding the paper money wrinkled in his hand and awkwardly pushing it into his pocket and taking it out again, he said, "*Sim, senhor.*" I drew up in front of my lodging, stopped the truck, and turned to him.

"Well then, José, get out now."

He did absolutely nothing, he just sat and shook his head back and forth, looking at me.

I repeated, "Well, get out."

And there he sat.

"For God's sake, José, get out! You're through and that's that!"

He answered, "*Sim, senhor,*" but he made no move.

Then I shook hands with him, I gave him my old hat, and still he stayed. I shook hands with him again and gave him a pair of my old shoes. He still did not go, so I sat there too. To my relief the houseboy from the guesthouse of the geologist where I was staying came out. He tried to explain to José that this was the end of our association and he had to leave. Then a great deal of conversation ensued between them and finally the other boy in broken English explained to me that José did not want to leave his master.

I said, "Tell José I'm going back to the States across the big water and I cannot take him with me."

To that José replied that he had decided he wanted to go with me just the same.

"Don't be foolish, José, you have a wife and children."

They didn't seem to matter in the least to him.

I continued, "José, I'm staying for two more days. To-morrow morning at six o'clock you go out to the house where you are going to work. As a special favor to you, you do not have to stay there overnight like the other houseboys. Just be sure you arrive there at six o'clock and before I go away, you come over here once more and say good-by."

José shook his head, hesitated for a long while, looked at me, shook his head again, and said, "*Sim, senhor,*" then haltingly walked away.

The next morning after breakfast as I walked out I immediately noticed that the truck was spotlessly clean, polished again like it always was before, and when I opened the door, which was locked throughout the night, on the rubber floor mat in the cab a small pool of water remained. What was that? It hadn't rained. How had it happened? Then I realized that my faithful José must have got up early, very early, maybe three or four o'clock in the morning, and walked for miles from his little hut far outside of Nova Lisboa in order to wash my truck, and then afterward to go to his new place of employment. I did not see him that day, but the following morning I noticed that he did the same thing again.

My last afternoon in Nova Lisboa I sold the truck, and evening found me at the railroad station. I had almost an hour before train time and was encumbered with a mountain of luggage, gear, and equipment. The Portuguese officials politely hovered over me, becoming entangled in their inevitable red tape and frantically labeling baggage and stamping passports.

I emerged at last onto the tiny platform where the customary excitement prevailed. Portuguese and natives, white and black were mingled and babbling in their respective tongues, at times drowned out by the tooting of the engine pulling and pushing a string of cars with no obvious purpose back and forth along the same stretch of narrow-gauge track. My Portuguese and other white friends had arrived for final good-bys and we stood chatting together. As I was shaking hands right and left while natives pushed and jostled from all directions, a shrill whistle blew. "All aboard!" I got into the train.

I missed José. Where is he? He must come to see me off.

As I looked out the window of my compartment, there was José pushing his way through the crowd toward the slowly moving train with something tucked under his arm. When he drew nearer to the train and walked along, he lifted up to the window and held out a *matabis*, a live chicken, thrusting it into my hands with his hesitant, childish, and sincere smile. Farewell token, *senhor!*

What can one do with a boy like that?

The wheels were clicking, another whistle blew, and as things were moving, fading, the rhythmic *tum-ta-ta, tum-ta-ta*, like a distant drum from the faraway bush, was calling, calling again.

INDEX

279